RELIGIOUS DRAMA:
ENDS AND MEANS

Harold Ehrensperger

Abingdon Press   NASHVILLE   NEW YORK

MANUFACTURED BY THE PARTHENON PRESS AT
NASHVILLE, TENNESSEE, UNITED STATES OF AMERICA

FOR

Winifred Ward whose life has established
a standard of excellence which is seen
in her work in creative dramatics and
children's theatre

Robert Scott Steele whose life and work have
exemplified the values to which this book
is dedicated

FOREWORD

This book by Harold Ehrensperger is possibly the most important publication in the recent past in the field of religious drama. Harold Ehrensperger was one of the most creative spirits in the church. A lifelong love of the theater, including a college friendship with many important persons who became influential in the theater, gave him acquaintance and access to resources seldom available to persons interested in reflecting on the religious vocation of the theater. It is appropriate that the Board of Discipleship and the Board of Higher Education and Ministry of The United Methodist Church make possible this second edition of *Religious Drama: Ends and Means* so that a new generation of students may profit from the imagination and intelligence of Harold Ehrensperger.

Those of us who knew him remain under the spell of his excitement and his hope for the church. It is in that spirit that this publication is presented.

F. THOMAS TROTTER

PREFACE

Radical changes have occurred in the past ten years in all aspects of drama and the theater. What were once considered absolute norms for the definition of a play are now obsolete. At the present time there is little that can be declared sacrosanct. Probably at no time in the history of modern drama have so many different forms and nonforms been present at the same time. All aspects of the expression of the dramatic in the church have also come under new scrutiny.

The changing forms of art enhance its subject matter. Forms of drama may change, but the fascination of communicating with characters as they come alive on a stage or platform, or anywhere for that matter, endures. It is as old as mankind and as young as the child who first begins to act. The guise under which the emotions of persons interact may change, but the interpersonal relationships do not. The form of drama, whatever it may be, can be its distinguishing characteristic as art—its subject matter is always the same.

The relatively superficial material given in this short book is intended as a set of working suggestions for amateurs who are not ashamed of being so. These are people who delight in using means to achieve dramatic ends. They are not endeavoring to be professional in any sense; they are merely attempting to do the best possible job with the best possible assistance. The equivalent in music is the person who enjoys playing an instrument never expecting to be professional or the painter who delights in working, feeling no inferiority that he is not "exhibited." To work in these fields may be the genesis of a professional career or the inspiration to continue training, but for the most part in

the church its value is that of presenting life in one of its most appeal-
ing and effective art forms. It is fun in the finest sense!

People who can play together can grow together. Drama allows us
to come out of our narrow selves, to be part of a whole. This *whole*
is the play, the production, the audience; it is a process of maturation.
The purpose of formal drama in the church is not to teach (whatever
that may mean in our present educational upheaval, but it is, in Henri
Gheon's words, "to delight,"—to delight in aspects of life that can be
made impressive through dramatic means. In this book production of
drama in the church does not refer to the use made in New York and
other large cities of church auditoriums as theaters, although this may
be more intelligent play than bingo games. Our concern is with a
creative activity that achieves the highest possible enjoyment in the
process itself and in the reaction to the process.

A play which is a work of art has its own truth, and it must be re-
created and judged in the light of this truth. As a created object it awaits
interpretative insights from the mind of the director to give it actualization in physical space and time. The good play, effectively rendered,
captures attention and holds an audience in response. The play may
concern itself with a small segment of life, but this small segment, in one
way or another, has pertinency to a large framework of experience. It
allows one to walk with common people or with kings, to become one
with the great and small of humanity, and to have a renewed perspective on all of life. This is its greatest miracle. It may rid people of
differences which, despite their superficiality, may blind them to each
other. Morals, politics, and time and space distances may be perceived
in perspective and set aside through art which unites human beings on
an instinctual level—intimate, as well as universalizing.

Drama can succeed in uniting the whole person with the wholeness
of another human being, so that the result of the encounter may be
growth of many kinds. The subject matter of the play and the content
of the dramatic experience provide the bridge between the performer
and the audience or between one individual and another. By way of
this bridge communication that is profound and relatively total takes
place, fulfilling the original meaning of the word communication—a
sharing of suffering, happiness, wealth, property, and experience to the
point of unity. When sufficient life is made common through experienc-

ing drama, communication is restored to its original meaning—*communion.*

Drama then, like other arts, can keep us from wasting our minds and lives. It can lay its stern and uncompromising reality upon us, irritating and arousing us to the realization of a way that leads to the fulfillment of our destinies. This is reality—a form of teaching, to be sure—but it is the way we are least likely to think of as teaching in its traditional forms.

Detailed material on production is not included in this book. Excellent books on lighting, scenery, and costuming are now available. A small book of this nature can only cover surface suggestions that are important because of the place and purpose of the production. Furthermore, qualified people in all these fields are now found in most high schools, community theaters, and colleges. A few basic principles are given and an appeal is made for further work in workshops and other training centers. The great necessity is still for the understanding spirit and for imagination backed by competence. This will bring the joy that makes sense of any action.

HAROLD EHRENSPERGER

Gilmanton, New Hampshire
August, 1971

INTRODUCTION

Harold Adam Ehrensperger straddled two domains: theater and religion. His college days at Harvard brought him close to George Pierce Baker who founded the famed '47 Workshop. Some of Dr. Ehrensperger's (afterwards, HAE) classmates became America's leading playwrights, theater critics, and technicians. He was without a rival in being Professor Baker's favorite student and protegé; he was asked to remain at Harvard after his graduation, to be Professor Baker's assistant, and to work toward a graduate degree. HAE was drawn to all aspects of theater. He wrote plays and criticisms, directed plays, and supervised technical work. When Professor Baker left Harvard for Yale—Harvard would not build a theater so Yale did—he offered HAE a position on the faculty of the Yale School of Drama. But HAE had another idea for his life work. That had to do with religion.

But before he realized that he wished to work in religion, he did just about what all theatrically minded students do and went to New York City. He joined Stuart Walker in his Portmanteau Theatre. Walker began his career in the teens in New York City as the general stage manager for David Belasco. Walker's Portmanteau Theatre was an alternative to the show business of the commercial theater of New York City. The rationale for this theater was stated in its play programs: "The Portmanteau is a twentieth-century cart of Thespis, designed to travel, with its troupe and paraphernalia, from city to city, supplying entertainment in the market square [or its modern equivalent] or to such patrons as extend an invitation to their homes. Mechanically, it is a marvel of simplicity and completeness. And one discovers with glad surprise that its artistic product is as beautiful as its mechanical construction is deft." Hiram Kelly Moderwell, writing in *The Boston Transcript*, said, "The Portmanteau must prove one of the most definite and valuable contributions to imaginative staging and producing that America has yet seen." The group announced itself as "the theatre that comes to you," and its dedication was "to imagination, youth, and the eternal spirit of play." There was no other theater to which HAE could have given himself that so embodied his own

11

orientation to the mission of theater. Plays were produced in New York City and they were published there, but the ideal of the theater soon sent HAE to the hinterlands. In no time he founded the Indianapolis Little Theatre and became its director. The Indianapolis theater became a premiere locale for new Portmanteau plays.

Anna Brochausen, a beautiful and wise cousin of HAE's father and a high school teacher of English literature, had a special feeling for him when he was a boy and a man. She followed his career and was a mentor to him for as long as she lived. When he was a senior in high school, she took him to eastern colleges to select the one he wished to attend. She gave him an early acquaintance with and an affection for Shakespeare, Ibsen, Rostand, Galsworthy, Shaw, and British and American poets. Anna Brochausen felt that HAE's education was incomplete until he had a year's sojourn in Europe. He lived in Vienna for eight months absorbing the Max Reinhardt theatrical experiments; he also spent time in Berlin, Paris, Florence, and London. His year was spent learning all he could about the new developments in European theater. He had two unplanned encounters which were to be pivotal to his future. He was overwhelmed with the suffering of Germany as it tried to survive the aftermath of World War I. He was told the war years had provided easy living by comparison. Then he went to Assisi where he absorbed much of the spirit of St. Francis and found that his life could not be devoted solely to theater.

By the time he left Europe, he had decided on what he must do next: enroll as a student in Garrett Biblical Institute in Evanston, Illinois. The idea of serving in the conventional ministry had not brought about his decision to be a theological student and to take another degree, but to prepare himself to help people directly. Then as now, such training seemed to be the obvious place to begin.

Garrett is next door to the School of Speech of Northwestern University (the School of Speech offered all that was being offered at Northwestern in theater studies). So it was a short step for HAE to give courses in the School of Speech and the School of English. More influential upon him than his studies at Garrett was his meeting Ernest Freemont Tittle who was the minister of the First Methodist Church of Evanston. Dr. Tittle was not a man to tell HAE that he should turn his back on his love of the theater and take up preaching. Dr. Tittle was a brilliant, courageous, and liberal man. He prevailed upon HAE to work in drama at his church. He spoke HAE's language, and HAE became devoted to Dr. Tittle. So the tug-of-war between the influences of Professor Baker and Dr. Tittle was resolved. Once and for all, HAE chose against a career in professional theater and made his vocation religion and drama.

In Evanston HAE became the director of the Community Theater. Then he became the national executive secretary of the Drama League of America. He wrote and directed *The Spreading Flame* which began as "the Garrett pageant" and then became the official pageant celebrating the sesquicentennial of American Methodism. He headed the division of plays and pageants of The Methodist Episcopal Church. He published anthologies of plays which he thought were worth producing in churches. He was the editor of the *Little Theatre Monthly* and served on the editorial board of *Drama Magazine*. And from 1925 to 1942 he kept up his teaching at Northwestern. He stretched himself to cover not only two specializations but many. Somehow he managed to get over the nation to lecture to hundreds of community theater, campus, and church groups. He became a most sought-after lecturer. His lecture topics were: "The Current Theatrical Season"; "Behind the Scenes of a Changing Stage"; "The Theater as Art and Entertainment"; "Changing Aspects of the American Theater"; "Amateur and Professional Contributions to the Drama"; and "Drama in Religion."

We can be thankful that HAE was never the recipient of the sobriquet *Mr. Religious Drama*. But I was close enough to his talk, correspondence, and colleagues from 1940 on, to know that he was esteemed as *the* national authority in religion and drama. He was the pioneer in leading churches and national bodies of churchmen and churchwomen to recognize that drama could be a vital part of a ministering church. He never got into an eddy, as many of his students and followers did, of confining his orbit to drama in churches. For him drama was to be created in communities, on campuses, and, more recently, in out-of-doors regional pageants. He never stopped making regular pilgrimages to New York City and Europe to see the best theater he could find. In fact, he attended theater festivals around the world. In 1936 he was the tour leader for a group that attended a theater festival in Moscow.

When one's mind runs over the leaders in religion and drama for the last three decades, many of them seem to have fallen into either the

church or the theater camp. There have been church persons who have
felt drama is valuable enough to be nurtured in their churches. There
have been the professional religionists who have written plays for
churches. These playwrights of the church have had laudable intentions,
but frequently they have been lacking in theatrical knowledge, taste,
and ability. Much of what they have done has been "acceptable" as
long as it was shielded by church darkness. In a church one could
assume that an audience which knew little about religion and nothing
about drama would accept anything that was proffered under church
auspices. A play seemed to be a nice thing to have at Christmas and
Easter, and old-timers noted that a dramatic program in a church
seemed to interest the young people—and it could do no harm.

HAE would have none of this. He weathered the years of either
recalcitrant or wooden church professionals who thought that a play in
a church was the best choice for entertainment after a supper. The
drama that he knew and believed in was measured by a single standard
whether it took place in a church building or in a commercial, community, or university theater. He had no time for a simulation, in a
church basement, of the high school senior play or the most modish
comedy just off Broadway. For him, if drama were to be in the
church, it belonged in the church. It belonged as a substantial part of
the life of a church. It belonged in the main auditorium because it was
a dramatic work of religious significance and power. It was not to be
relegated as a hobby for those who otherwise never darkened the church
door. HAE brought the same aesthetic sensitivity—and sanity—to all
drama that he encountered or for which he was responsible.

The difference that characterized the work that he fostered was
blatantly discernible. Even though it was a drama in the church, it
had to be founded upon good theatrical principles. After all, he knew
dramaturgy as well as theater. Professor Baker invited him to spend
a summer with him in New Hampshire to assist with the writing of
his book *Dramatic Technique*. This book was the bible of dramaturgy
for a generation of our finest playwrights. Professor Baker had the job of
being a *play doctor* to the legitimate theater of New York City when it
was ailing. He and HAE made countless trips to see rehearsals and
advise playwrights and directors about changes that might be made to
improve productions.

If one did not know HAE but knew only about his schooling, it would be natural to assume that he fell into the camp of the theater enthusiast working in church drama, but he did not. He managed to have the respect of theater-minded persons working in church drama because he didn't need to say much for it to become evident that he knew more about theater than they. So he could succeed in wooing them from theatrical shenanigans. Scores of persons learned from him the changes that were needed to make theater at home in a church. While his footing was sure in drama, it was also sure in religion, but his religious values remained less changed than his thinking about drama and theater. Occasionally in the late forties, *motive*, which he founded and edited for ten years, was critized by some Union theological students for being insufficiently preoccupied with the theologies of Karl Barth, Emil Brunner, and Reinhold Niebuhr. These popular theologians of the late forties did not appeal to HAE as much as they appealed to some urban theological students. HAE's theology remained liberal and related to the New Testament and the social gospel. So for some students, his theology was passé. His religious thinking and values were permeated by idealist thinkers, philosophers, theologians, and an occasional rabbi and priest. The ideals of liberal Christianity never became irrelevant for him, even though many times they were not to be achieved immediately. An *impossible* ideal would take just a little longer to be accepted.

Religion and drama for HAE were not theatrical activities within a church which had little to do with the total ministry, religious living, and ethical goals which should characterize church life. While an interest in religion and drama places one foot of a person in the religion camp and the other in the theater camp, HAE kept his head above both groups and fought for their sensitive and intelligent unification. He was not inclined to knock either, but certainly he did not lend his interest to bogged-down camps. There was sufficient understanding and security in his ministry to realize that individuals in both camps often were there, because, like the rest of us, they have problems. He knew that some people only used the church to compensate for the lack of a career in theater. But he saw that if a religionist could latch onto a good play, that person might outgrow dramatized sermons.

HAE was aware of the conflicts that exist when persons are limited in their knowledge of theater and religion so that they could not comprehend their need of different means to achieve similar goals. The goals of both art and religion are preventing the waste of lives, saving and protecting life, nurturing the good so that it may grow, depicting and celebrating truth, goodness, and beauty. Dramatic art and religion can do this. He understood that a play, like religion, should be a source of inspiration to an audience, but that a good play is not a polemic. Its aim is not to prevail upon a viewer to make an immediate ethical decision. When a play does that, it undermines the art of the theater and becomes propaganda. A play's reason for being is to be a good play. It reveals something that may have been forgotten, hidden, or not understood. It makes visible and audible what previously was not seen or heard. The use of any and all arts in the church does this and justifies them as ministerial means.

The title of HAE's first book, *Conscience on Stage*, stated his thinking about the use of drama in the church. Conscience makes the difference between persons and nonpersons. Consciences are quickened when persons are caught in conflict with themselves or other persons. When the heightened consciences of persons are made clear for all to listen and watch on a stage (or in the street, club, classroom, or church), thinking and feeling may be born or reborn and visions of a better way of life may emerge. The meeting of consciences results in dramatic experiencing. This has been what our greatest dramatists, from Sophocles to Brecht, have done for us. HAE had to fight to get his publisher to accept the title, *Conscience on Stage*. That title was thought to be difficult, even abstruse, and would not easily lead church persons to a book that was intended for them. Labeling was what the publisher wanted, and HAE agreed to the labeling of his second book, *Religious Drama*, but he insisted on tacking on *Ends and Means*. The "ends" are religious and aesthetic living. They are the emancipated life, the illuminated life, the celebrating life. The "means" are well conceived, written, and produced dramas that have theatrical power, that are created for churches and offered in churches.

HAE's contribution to drama and religion could make both George Pierce Baker and Ernest Freemont Tittle say, "Well done, Harold! You had the will, vision, and talent to save yourself from being our mere acolyte. You were driven to do unique and pioneering work—work that neither of us was doing, nor ever could have done."

ROBERT STEELE, *Boston*, 1974

CONTENTS

17

PART TWO

    A. DRAMA AS CELEBRATION
       Christmas
       Lent and Easter

    B. EDUCATION THROUGH DRAMATIC PRODUCTION

    C. DRAMA AS RECREATION

    A. DRAMATIC WORSHIP
       The Leader of Worship
       Ways to Dramatic Effectiveness
       Dramatic Unity
       Dramatic Prayer

    B. MUSIC IN WORSHIP
       Dramatic Leadership
       Dramatic Timing

    C. USING THE CHANCEL AS A PLAYING AREA

PART THREE

    A. THE DIRECTOR AND DIRECTING

    B. CASTING

    C. THE PROMPTBOOK

    D. THE ACTOR AND ACTING

    A. ORGANIZING FOR PRODUCTION

The three laws governing religious drama

We always have control over the means and never the ends. The end grows out of the means. As the means, so the end. The means may be likened to a seed; the end to a tree. And there is the same inviolable connection between the means and the ends as there is between the seed and the tree. If one takes care of the means the end will take care of itself, and the realization of the goal is in exact proportion to that of the means.

> —G. N. Dhiwan, The Political Philosophy of Mahatma Gandhi (Bombay: The Popular Book Depot, 1946), p. 49.

This is the first law of religious drama

The distinction of means and ends arises in surveying the course of a proposed line of action, a connected series in time. The end is the last act thought of; the means are acts to be performed prior to it in time. To reach an end, we must take our mind off from it and attend to the act which is next to be performed. We must make that the end.

> —John Dewey, Human Nature and Conduct (New York: Henry Holt & Company, 1922), p. 34.

This is the second law of religious drama

There is only one means and there is only one end: the means and the end are one and the same thing. There is only one end: the genuine good; and only one means: this, to be willing to use those means which genuinely are good—but the genuine good is precisely the end. In time one distinguishes between the two and considers that the end is more important than the means. One thinks that the end is the main thing and demands of one who is striving that he reach the end. He need not be so particular about the means. Yet this is not so, and to gain an end in this fashion is an unholy act of impatience.

> —Purity of Heart by Sören Kierkegaard. Translated by Douglas E. Steere. Used by permission of Harper & Brothers.

This is the third and final law of religious drama

Part one

Chapter I

THE MEANING OF THE DRAMATIC

BECAUSE ITS RAW MATERIAL IS THE TOTAL HUMAN BEING, DRAMA IS THE most alive of all the arts. Human beings are presented to other human beings in situations of movement, action, and change. Drama is life in motion seen at times of especial significance. The dramatist puts movement and action on a stage and holds it there until we have had a good look at it. It is housed in a building, fixed in a frame, or held at a distance so that it is sufficiently arrested for us to grasp it. By way of dramatization we get some beginning, middle, and ending out of segments of ongoing and ephemeral life. This view of a selection from life in action enables us to see the extent of our own aliveness or deadness and consequently to walk away from an experience of drama more alive than we have ever been before.

The dramatic performance is primarily visual, but it cannot achieve maximum effectiveness without support from the spoken word. Verbal language announces the meaning of movement and action; also it illumines and clarifies. Decisions resulting from the experience of meeting life in action are arrived at before an audience. Speech divides the ambiguous from the nonambiguous. The words of a drama help man to make and transmit man's decisions. Therefore, drama is a unique art form because it presents life in action culminated in decision-making which makes it possible for this action to lead to more life in action.

Drama is also unique in that its substance is embodied in flesh, blood, bone, and voice. The artist is a creator of symbols. The dramatic artist uses symbols that are human beings. Symbols in painting, literature, and music are created of a nonhuman substance. Therefore, more interpretation is needed for these art forms. The drama speaks to the audience most directly. We in the audience are met directly by the minds, expressions, gestures, and decisions of the performers. Their acts and decisions readily become ours. The substance from which the symbols are created is the same substance of the audience. Performers and audience are one in the raw material and the subject matter of the drama. Contrasted with other art forms little translation or interpretation of the symbols is necessary for the performers and the audience to participate as an organic whole in perceiving the portend of the life depicted in the drama. Readily we see, hear, feel, understand, believe or disbelieve, and accept or reject what the dramatist says to us about life.

Because of the closeness of experience in the drama to that of the audience, because of its directness and immediacy, it can be easily forgotten that drama is not reality. Drama, more than other art forms, can reach us in ways that seem astonishingly real and true. Yet drama must never be confused with or strive to pass for reality. If this happens drama ceases to be drama and its value is lost. No matter how real the performers may seem or how lifelike their problems, actions, and decisions, drama to be drama must always be the illusion of reality. This nonreal, illusory, and artificial nature of drama explains its power, worth, and necessity for us. Great drama is never a record or photograph of ourselves but a re-creation of ourselves by way of the mind of the dramatist. This allows us to see ourselves from his point of view.

Drama exists only in performance. Because its life is fabricated and fictionalized, selected and organized, contrived and controlled, it can happen only in the shape and form of a created object—the play. It is not something we encounter on the street; it is the creative work of the dramatist. It does not exist in the mind of the reader of a script. Its existence is in the tangible, physical life in action mounted on a stage. It is a production that has emerged from expanding, compressing, and arbitrarily creating. The play is an artistic expression that has reality, and it is more real than reality itself. The reality of a play is fabricated from the most meaningful and significant moments of many moments, of many lives, of millions of words. It is a created nexus of movement, crisis, and language which has the power to condition the future living of those who experience the play. By way of living persons who interact upon each other in such a way that they interact with the audience it unfolds a story. The participating experience of the audience is so important that drama can be complete and alive only in the presence of an audience. A play is designed for performance, and it is born when it gathers more life to itself by way of the response of an audience. Response resulting from the sharing of the experience is integral to the reality of the drama. This sharing of the meaning of the play by the actors with the audience provides the essence of drama. The spectator ceases to be spectator as the play gets under way, because he projects himself imaginatively into a participation with the destiny of the characters in the performance.

This sharing takes place by empathy. A member of the audience does not feel merely sympathetic for the characters and identify himself as an observer of the crisis or problem; he is actually *in* the crisis to such an extent that the crisis is his, the problem is his, the dilemmas and potentialities of the characters are his, and the actors are himself. His projection into them and their introjection into him result in the experience being an organic whole. The response of the audience may be hisses or bravoes. The response that is the result of the sharing, whether it be rejection or acceptance, makes the miracle of drama take place. By this empathic experience, according to Aristotle, as well as to contemporary psychological thought, man is purged of the emotions of pity and fear. To this classic concept of catharsis and its function in the theater John Gassner adds "enlightenment" to pity and fear. "In tragedy," he writes, "there is always a precipitate of final enlightenment —some inherent, cumulative, realized, understanding . . . a clear comprehension of what was involved in the struggle, an understanding of cause and effect, a judgment on what we have witnessed, and our induced state of mind that places it above the riot of passion." [1]

The spectator is so much a participant that he is emotionally aroused and later intellectually able to rise above passion to make a judgment. The director of a dramatic performance is aware of this end to be sought; he is involved in the action on the stage, and yet he maintains an awareness of the feeling and enlightenment of the audience so that he may direct the moment when passion is transformed to judgment. He is responsible for the final enlightenment following the understanding of the cause and effect working in the play which will bring about a verdict in the lives of the audience. The emotions shared by the audience, the purging that has taken place, the enlightenment, the residue of judgment, and the decision making that takes place are culminated in a re-creative experience. By way of the experience cast in a creation of the dramatist, the member of the audience experiences its re-creation in and for himself; this constitutes the aesthetic experience of drama. The efficacy of the play is derived from the depth and extent of the sharing of the performance. The member of the audience leaves the theater as a re-created human being. Because of the creative work of the dramatist and performers the audience becomes changed human beings. Participants have been re-created, and the power and permanence of this re-creation is the yardstick for the measurement of the greatness of the dramatic experience.

The form of the drama from which this re-creative experience is distilled is called a play. The root meaning of "play" is illusion; literally, the word means "in play" (*illuderi*). Drama happens when we are in play.

From infancy play is vital for us. We cannot grow into human beings without an abundance of play in our lives. It must go on from birth to death. Children play being grown-up. By way of the enlightenment they receive from play, they learn, experience, and grow into maturing human beings. Child's play is acting which has a social function.[2] It is a voluntary and craved activity which incorporates movement, action, conflict, and language. Play is fabricated from tensions which result from the eagerness to achieve the ends in view. Play has form and rules. In play a boy may stab his sister with a rubber knife, but play is over when the weapon ceases to be an imaginary one. Play remains play as long as it is of an illusory and imaginative nature. Masks and disguises are essential to play. They represent the creation of an image or symbol or the realization of a desired appearance which substitutes for the real. ("Only the drama, because of its intrinsically functional character, its quality of being actions, remains permanently linked to play." [3])

Advanced chronological age does not take away the need for play. Adults also must play, participate in make-believe, and open floodgates of re-creative activity. Because of this need we have had art with us from the beginning of time. Art is man's play. We do not find any people anywhere at anytime whose culture is devoid of some kind of expression that seems to serve no function other than art for the sake of art. Much activity serves religious needs, but we also find decoration and artistic expression that serve no function other than the need to express. Art, therefore, is no luxury to be engaged in in times of leisure or peace. It is a vital part of life, whenever we find it.

Dromenon, from which the word "drama" comes, was something acted in a performance or contest. It focuses our attention on the play as action, as illusion, and as expression of our enjoyment. The play, the form of drama, therefore is an illusion of life which is acted out as if it were actuality. It shows action rather than talks about it. It does not paint life but sets it before us. It shows man's interior nature working itself out as an objective fact.

"Man's interior nature working itself out" indicates the uniqueness of dramatic expression as contrasted to theatrical expression, if by theatrical expression is meant spectacle and the spectacular. Louis Adamic suggests that the drama of things is the truth of things to the extent that if one perceives the drama of a thing one perceives the truth of it. To write truthfully, then, is to write dramatically. The dramatic is our interior nature expressing itself truthfully in the apparent symbols of human beings.

To write truthfully, and therefore to write dramatically, means that the theatrical may be a blind alley. The production aids of lighting, scenery, costuming, and makeup may enhance a dramatic presentation, but they are aids to help create and sustain the illusion. Drama can come into being with a minimum of these so that sometimes by an excess or misuse of production aids drama is obliterated.

Theatrical is identified with theater—an institution that has emerged in most civilizations. Since the beginning of recorded time, in every culture the essentially dramatic of existential experience has sought a place where it may be presented. The production aids of theater are largely the results of the needs of the place where performances occur. The play can come alive both in the theater or outside the theater; in fact the miracle can happen anywhere. Strolling players who performed in the open, the masques presented in English and French courts, and space-staging which uses all sorts of playing areas are evidence that a theater building is not necessary. The truth of the idea, theme, characters, and conflict can be so potent that the audience may be unaware of the presence or absence of aids. Drama can exist without the theater but the theater cannot exist without drama.

For the fullest enjoyment of theater, however, all production aids may be of value, and for pageantry and spectacle they are essential. They can enhance and enrich the power of the dramatic experience. Their cumulative effect lends excitement that only theater can have. Yet, despite their value, they remain auxiliary to the necessities of drama as an art form. The theatrical in the drama is present to the extent that it is essential. Production aids are to be used to the extent that the dramatic form may have its finest support and expression, so that it may best communicate to performers and the audience.

The theater may be a vehicle for the presentation of truthful and spiritual subject matter, but frequently it is an institution surviving on trivia. To make it more marketable bits and pieces of showmanship used for titillation are tacked onto a play. When great drama is presented in the theater, or away from the theater, the subject matter is so integral that it cannot be tampered with. It is an entity, a reality in itself. Great drama should not be victimized by peripheral theatrics or showmanship. The uncompromised taste and judgment of the writer is combined with the taste and judgment of the director in order to create a vicarious experience for members of the audience. The production aids of the theater, along with the producer, the director, and the actors, are tools for the realization of the intention and purpose of the dramatist.

A play which is a work of art has its own truth, and it must be recreated and judged in the light of its truth. As a created object it awaits interpretative insights from the mind of the director to give it actualization in physical space and time. The good play effectively rendered captures attention and holds an audience in an attitude of responding. The play may concern itself with a small segment of life, but this small segment, in some way or another, has pertinency to a large framework of experience. It allows one to walk with common men and kings, to become one with the great and small of humanity, and to have a recreated perspective on all of life. The play, like other art forms, rids men of differences which, despite their superficiality, may blind them to each other. Morals, politics, and time and space distances may be perceived in perspective and set aside by way of art which unites human beings on an instinctual, intimate, and universalizing level.

This responsibility for perceiving truthfully in order that we may present and experience truthfully is not limited to dramatists of the past. To get the truth of a French dramatist of the twentieth century, we must see him and hold him in those limiting aspects of his culture and milieu. To judge the contemporary playwright of Japan in the context of American drama or vice versa is absurd and false.

The greatness of drama lies in its capacity to contribute to the spiritual growth of man. It can succeed in uniting the whole man with the whole of another man, so that the result of the encounter will be growth of many kinds. The subject matter of the play and the content of the dramatic experience provide the bridge between the performer and the audience or between man and man. By way of this bridge communication that is profound and relatively total takes place. Communication that takes place fulfills the original meaning of the word "communication," which is the sharing of suffering, wealth, property, and experience until they become one. Ben Jonson spoke of "the thousands who communicate our loss." When sufficient life is made common by way of the experiencing of drama, communication is restored to its original meaning, "communion." The consequence of persons meeting persons in such a way that actors and audience commune results in their being transformed into a community. When one feels this is happening in a theater, a school, a church, or under a tent, he can know he has experienced the miracle of drama. When drama communicates truth and results in spiritual growth, revelation and rediscovery of meanings and values in life are taking place.

Drama, then, like other arts, is that which keeps us from wasting our minds, energies, and lives. It shows us a way to a better way and puts us to work saving what is worthy of being saved that we and others possess. Because the dramatic experience has shown how the redemption of life takes place we are saved from the stupidities and losses of our past selves. Drama, both in and out of the theater, can lay its stern and uncompromising reality upon us, irritating and arousing us to the realization of the way we must go in doing our duty to fulfill our destinies. This is a religious experience.

The danger of theater is greater than that of other art forms. When the raw material and subject matter are one—that is, the human being is the vehicle of the art form—reality of the human being and reality of the dramatic experience come threateningly close. They so mingle that the hazard of substitution of realities is precarious, and it is fatal to both when fusing exists. The creators of dramatic experience may unknowingly substitute their reality in life-as-it-is for life-in-the-theater or in dramatic experience. This paves the road for an escape from reality. When this happens drama has lost its value, and its practitioners are our enemies. The unrealized perfection we can experience by way of the drama is confused with perfected reality and the illusion becomes delusion. Drama and theater fail us when they become so satisfying that we are content. The power of the drama lies in its capacity to arouse, to stimulate, and to irritate.

Drama shows us what ought to be. It is on the move toward perfection of the individual and the social order. It presents the will of man in conflict with the yet-to-be-created or the already-created which is destroying man. This is also its miracle. By way of dramatic experience we can have a sense of fulfillment and delight. It can be so powerful and so wonderful we are jolted when the curtain comes down and the spell is broken. This hypnotic experience of how life could be or what it is yet to be, despite its being made today frequently in negative statements, can carry us off into constructive or destructive fantasy-making. Drama can fill or empty us. No other art form can so bewitch or inspire us.

The purpose of this book is to explore ways in which drama can find its deepest meanings and realize them in dramatic terms. When this happens drama will have religious meaning wherever it is born.

Notes

[1] J. A. Withey, "Action in Life and in Drama," *The American Educational Theatre Journal*, X, N. 3 (October, 1958) 234, quoting John Gassner, *European Theories of the Drama*, ed., Barrett H. Clark (Rev. ed.; New York: Crown Publishers, 1947), p. 550.

[2] For a full treatment of the play theory of life see Johan Huizinga, *Homo Ludens, A Study of Play Element in Culture* (Boston: Beacon Press, 1955).

[3] *Ibid.*, p. 144.

Chapter II

THE PLAY

A. Structure

A PLAY IS THE ACTUALIZATION OF A SEGMENT OF LIFE IN A TIME SEQUENCE brought to life by characters whose action and speech are relevant to the crisis moment in which they have been caught. The form of the play can be defined by episodes that are called scenes and acts. These are usually arranged in an order of rising action to culminate in a climax.

Contemporary playwrights are not overly concerned about traditional techniques of playwriting. They are, nevertheless, still concerned about the adequate realization of the story in a form that uses action and dialogue and that has a beginning and rising action culminating in an end when the tension or tensions giving rise to dramatic action are at least temporarily resolved. That many contemporary plays do follow this formula is only evidence of the vitality and freshness of the dramatists.

Aristotle in the *Poetics* suggests six components of a good play. He gives as his leading argument a worthy theme. This can often be expressed in a sentence which might be called a topic sentence. It is the idea of the play, the subject, the dramatic situation, the idea behind the tension situation that is being treated. The use of the word "worthy" is significant because it defines the subject matter in a particular way. For Aristotle tragedy has to have a sublime, elevated theme.

The second characteristic of a good play is that it shall have convincing characters. By this is meant characters in which the audience can believe, whose semblance of reality is sufficiently apparent to make them convincing. In Greek drama the characters were likely to be legendary heroes or gods whom the audience knew. The dramatist was bound by this knowledge and had to use it convincingly.

The next component was a well-knit plot, which can be explained as

29

a plot that holds together, that is fastened by events which lead from one to the other so that the audience is kept interested and attentive. This is inherent in Aristotle's concept of the unity of action.

The concept of memorable diction is less appreciated today because we would probably not use the word memorable. We would suggest that the diction in a good play ought to be characteristic, that it ought to belong to the characters. This does not mean that it cannot be memorable. Unfortunately our idea of memorable diction is likely to be related to its use by Shakespeare or one of the other great classical dramatists. So it should, but it should also cause us to look for the approximation of this in all plays. Too much of our dialogue is undistinguished and commonplace.

Contributing melody may mean either the melody of the words themselves as they are spoken or the use of melody accompanying the words. Just to hear Greek spoken gives an idea of what melody could have meant. Music was used in the theater as an expression of the mood and feeling of the play. We have revived music to express emotion which words alone may be unable to do. Along *with* action and dialogue, not merely as accompanying action and dialogue, music contributes to the play. Our stage has been the poorer because we have lost the melody of language as well as the melody of music.

Aristotle's last component is attendant spectacle. This allows for spectacle as an inherent aspect of theater. One can readily understand this in the Greek theater. Its size, its needs for physical proportions in the actors, and for the use of masks all lent the air of spectacle to the performance.

A play is an art form—a form which can be described in terms as distinctive as those in architecture, graphic arts, or music. It is a form that is characterized by dramatic limitations prescribed by the tension which the writer is treating.

The tensions that cause dramatic situations may be between the "selves" in a man, between what is often called his "higher" and his "lower" self, between the positive and the negative, the healthy and the unhealthy forces in his own personality. Tensions also arise in man between his will and that of another because of antagonisms, ambitions, et cetera. A play can also show the tension between a man and his ultimate destiny, between what he is and what he wants to be.

In Greek drama the tension was often between a man and his fate—

as, for example, in *Oedipus Rex*—or between a man, however great, and his gods—*Prometheus Bound*. Most contemporary plays actualize the tensions between men seen in social situations in the home, in business, or in politics. We are no longer able to blame the gods or our fates for the dilemmas through which our tensions are expressed. Psychology has explained these in terms of variations from norms and in conditionings which can be understood and dealt with. Many of our tensions arise today out of ignorance of their causes or out of our unwillingness to face them and seek their resolution. Drama uses these to the best advantage.

Characters

Tensions are always expressed through characterization in emotionally charged situations even when their origin has been intellectually conceived. Shaw "discusses" many things in his plays, but conversations on any questions are never dramatically interesting until they are emotionally expressed. Characterization simply means the way in which the dramatist has shaped the persons who are the people of his story.

In ancient drama the characters were usually well-known figures. They acted according to their known characteristics—the hero like the personage known in the story, the king according to the legend which has been built around him. All kings had much in common. Any minute differentiation in character that made for idiosyncracy was practically unknown. It could not be communicated under the conditions of the classic theater.

Later drama was to present persons as types; this is seen to an excellent advantage in the commedia dell' arte of Italy and in the morality plays of the Continent and England. The morality plays used characters that represented moral qualities or conditions or outstanding characteristics of human beings—vices and virtues. Some of the more recent plays of the contemporary stage are also endeavoring to focus attention on qualities and situations rather than on the idiosyncracies of the characters.

Some of the post-World War I dramatists, particularly writers like Georg Kaiser, Elmer Rice, and a few of the Soviet playwrights, named their characters as numbers—for example, Mr. Zero—or by the generic title Man, Woman, Child. They were able to universalize them so that they became symbols rather than individuals. They often represented classes of men, such as the manual worker or the white-collar worker, with the characterization conceived in broad strokes with little sense of a particular person. This seemed good for social drama where conflicts concerned classes of people rather than individuals. It served certain kinds of drama which were written to convict on social issues. Too much individualization in character may cause the audience to "look at" a person and to miss the overall social meaning. It is often easier for the audience to identify itself with broader characteristics of mankind or with social groups rather than with individuals in the group. Too often the audience can escape identification by insisting that the character is peculiar, a unique person, and therefore unrecognizable. (Witness reaction to the characters in Tennessee Williams' plays.) There is no empathy when this happens, no identification, no realization of "There, but for the grace of God, go I."

The epic theater of Bertolt Brecht takes another interesting point of view by distrusting the emotions when they are used merely for the sake of emotions. The spectator does not experience empathy, although he must be awakened in order to make decisions. The theater, for Brecht, communicates knowledge by *putting action in front of the spectator*. Each scene in a Brecht play exists for itself, and its social reality determines what man thinks. These concepts have aroused the contemporary dramatist and have made Brecht a highly controversial figure. The traditional idea of the play has been challenged by an extraordinarily intelligent playwright and man of the theater.

In the Renaissance the figures in a play began to take on real characteristics identified by their individuality. Hamlet was a prince; he acted like a prince, and everyone knew him as a prince. But what a unique person Hamlet was! What a different sort of prince! Characters in tragedy were usually of the upper classes or of royalty. Not until a century after the renaissance of drama in England were tragedies written about ordinary men, about the common man.

American drama today is not only the drama of the common man; it is also the drama of man exhibited with idiosyncracies, with evidences of difference from rather than likeness to his fellow men. So far has this gone in some realistic plays that audiences are likely to leave a performance asking where such characters came from or where they live? Are they not the pathetic inventions of the diseased mind of the dramatist? Is the theater a clinic for psychological analysis? We have so individualized characters, so made them into freaks, that there seems to be little universality in them. They are not the common man because we have nothing in common with them—that is, unless we are ready to admit that all mankind is sick and that we are freaks instead of individuals.

The dramatist is limited by the need to introduce his characters speedily and yet thoroughly. A person appears and by his speech and action assumes a character. As persons act and speak in a play, their characters are revealed. They must be true to their characters, and the dramatist is compelled to make them "develop" because they are the people they are. The inexperienced writer is likely to be guilty of oversimplification of character and of thereby making people fit an idea or fulfill a role. When an actor begins to bring a character to life the audience can readily see whether the dramatist has been honest, whether he has made this man or this woman speak and act as they do because they are the people they are. Development of character calls for *clarification* as well as revelation.

Careless dramatists are likely to oversimplify all characterization—a minister has certain characteristics, he speaks and acts like a minister; a doctor, a teacher, or a lawyer all speak and act like the professional figures they represent. This leads to caricature rather than characterization. Perhaps the reason why such caricatures are disappearing from drama is that they are disappearing from the contemporary scene. There is no typical doctor, apothecary, lawyer, and—lingeringly and slowly on the way out—no typical teacher or minister.

Characters are distinguished by appearance and by speech. What they are is revealed and clarified by what we call their characteristics—their appearance, speech, and action. What they are outwardly, however, is the revelation of what they are beneath the surface. The dramatist must know his characters thoroughly, so that he can let them reveal themselves through what they look like, what they say, and what they do. This, as has been suggested, is a process of clarification as well as revelation.

Plot

Characters are related to each other and reveal themselves through what is called a plot—the structure of the story that has enmeshed the characters. A plot is a contrived, connected narrative.

Plot is revealed at the beginning of a play by the exposition made possible through characters in a given situation. The exposition is executed by means of characters who may be a prologue or by any group of characters important to and integral to later, connected events in the story of the play. The dramatist must interest the audience at once. There is no opportunity in contemporary plays to lose time, to talk or act without motivation that leads directly into the tension situation with which the play deals. Greek plays used the chorus for exposition; Elizabethan playwrights often introduced minor characters to give information to the audience. All plays must tell the events that happened before the play began which lead up to the action of the play, so that the audience knows the circumstances of the action. They must know why the dramatist chose this beginning and why there could be no other.

Plot is introduced by the opening exposition to establish the beginning action and to introduce the people related to the action. It develops by revealing the tension, or what has been called the problem of the play. The development of the plot in most plays proceeds to a climax which usually has been foreshadowed by a series of crises. These crises build up to the heightened tension moment *to* which the plot moves and *from* which it moves to what we call the end. The end is merely the resolution of the main tension or problem that the plot has treated. It is not necessarily a solution of the problem although it may be. It is, however, the resolution of the particular tension, the settling for the moment, at least, of the problem that has been the basis of the plot.

Dialogue

Dialogue is manipulated conversation. It is conversation with a purpose. If one considered how much of his conversation is without any main purpose he would realize that when conversation is used for dialogue it must be cleaned up, condensed, and pointed. Our conversation is not ordinarily consciously pointed, and, therefore, it needs pruning to give it the compactness and direction necessary for a play.

Every word spoken in a play should have a necessary function. Words are active in a play just as bodily action is, and they constitute one of the distinguishing characteristics of drama. The function of dialogue, like that of action, is to move the plot forward and to reveal character. In what are often called "literary" plays dialogue takes on importance as poetry or prose, and the play may have literary as well as dramatic significance. The plays of Shakespeare, as well as those of T. S. Eliot, Sean O'Casey, and Christopher Fry of our own day, contain dialogue that is dramatically sound and yet strikingly effective as literature.

Obviously, good dialogue "belongs" to the character; it is characteristic of the person speaking it. It reveals the period of the play, the social status of the characters, and the geographical area from which they come. It is actually the most revealing thing about the characters.

B. Types of Plays

Dramatic form has been distinguished by four major types: Tragedy, comedy, farce, and melodrama. None is easy to define exactly, and none is a tight compartment which excludes other forms that are closely related. At various times and with various types of plays, dramatic historians have distinguished plays as histories, as problem plays, as "serious" plays that are not tragedies, as tragicomedies, as farce-comedies, as farce-melodramas, and as burlesque. The four main forms do call for a fifth—a play which is not strictly speaking a comedy and yet is not a tragedy. This type of play is serious and usually centers around a problem. More than likely it is a serious play that is motivated by characters in a situation which is not intrinsically the stuff of comedy and yet, at the same time, is not tragic. We have no name for such a type of play. It is often referred to just as "a drama." Shakespeare's *Merchant of Venice*, Ibsen's *The Doll's House*, Shaw's *Saint Joan*, and T. S. Eliot's *The Cocktail Party* are interesting examples of serious plays that are not strictly speaking comedy. Even the four main forms have been defined differently in various periods of the history of the drama.

Tragedy [1]

The oldest and most often quoted definition of tragedy is that of Aristotle in his *Poetics*: "Tragedy is an imitation of an action that is serious, complete, and of a certain magnitude; in language embellished with each kind of artistic ornament, the several kinds being found in separate parts of the play; in the form of action not of narrative; through pity and fear affecting the proper purgation of those emotions."

This classic definition covers the essential characteristics of all good drama—action, serious treatment, completion, certain magnitude of worth, good language, and empathy that causes the spectator to be purged especially of certain emotions. "Tragedy," says James H. Clay, "is a closed form. The last scene of a tragedy is not merely the establishment of balance; it marks an absolute terminus, to which a sequel is unthinkable." [2]

John Gassner suggests that in tragedy the characters play "for keeps" rather than for the audience. We have come to associate high seriousness, motivated human conduct having social as well as psychological causation, with tragedy. The calamity may be a means of "achieving significant revelations concerning character."

The conflict in a play that leads to tragic consequences is characterized by the quality of the antagonists and their proportions as men. When man is overcome so that he is defeated by evil forces against which he struggles his is a tragic fate. He may fight against his baser self; he may be in conflict with other men or with groups of men in society. He may combat powers higher than himself and be overcome by them. He may defy God and be defeated.

W. H. Auden said:

Greek tragedy is the tragedy of necessity; i.e., the feeling aroused in the spectator is "What a pity it had to be this way"; Christian tragedy is the tragedy of possibility, "What a pity it was this way when it might have been otherwise"; the hubris, which is the flaw in the Greek hero's character, is the illusion of a man who knows himself and believes that nothing can shake that strength, while the corresponding Christian sin of pride is the illusion of a man who knows himself weak but believes he can by his own efforts transcend that weakness and become strong.[3]

Tragedy used to concern itself only with lofty or exalted characters; the subject matter was also always lofty. The certain "magnitude" in Aristotle's definition is a different way of stating this. In a few plays before the nineteenth century and in most plays since Ibsen we have accepted ordinary people as persons of tragic dimensions. Some contemporary plays that are either intrinsically tragic or have overtones of tragedy of the ordinary man are Ibsen's Ghosts and Hedda Gabler; Strindberg's The Father; Tolstoi's The Power of Darkness; Gorki's The Lower Depths; O'Neill's The Hairy Ape, Desire Under the Elms, Mourning Becomes Electra, and The Ice Man Cometh; Giraudoux's Electra; Cocteau's The Infernal Machine; and Maxwell Anderson's Winterset and his Elizabethan trilogy.

Death is not inevitable in tragedy. To live may be more profoundly tragic than to die. One should not feel depressed after seeing a great tragedy. The exalted tragedy of Greek drama leaves one with a sense of the splendor of life, its magnificence and its stature. Tragedy demands great characters in significant tension situations.

Contemporary drama, as we can see from the plays we have just enumerated, has produced tragedies. These may be fewer in number because theater as escape or a commercial commodity demands pleasant plays that entertain in a particular way. In his play Marco Millions Eugene O'Neill has Marco voice the dilemma of the modern theater:

There's nothing better than to sit down in a good seat at a good play after a good day's work in which you know you've accomplished something, and after you've had a good dinner, and just take it easy and enjoy a good wholesome thrill or a good laugh and get your mind off serious things until it's time to go to bed.[4]

The popular problem play may have tragic implications, but its characters usually are not of the stature to be capable of tragic consequences. They are, more likely than not, little people caught up in little problems. Too often the theme capable of tragic proportions has become thesis. The characters are manipulated to satisfy the problem situation. The audience never gets to know or understand them—they are too busy working out the problem!

The lack of tragedy today may also be indicative of our surface living or of the numbing of sensitivity in a world where death and violence are accepted passively on both a small and large scale. The tragic consequences of Hamlet pale before the colossal potential tragedy of the atomic age. When one of today's major playwrights takes death and destruction for granted, having lived through two world wars—it is obvious that life for him can only be seen as ironic. The absurd, in Camus' phraseology, is characteristic of so much of life today. When a genuinely sensitive writer is able to get perspective on man as he is and as he might be he will almost be forced to write out of the anguish of his soul, and his drama is likely to be tragedy.

Comedy

No form of art is more vague in definition than comedy. To the plays of Aristophanes and to the most recent farce, the term comedy is applied. All plays except tragedy are broadly comedy. An examination of some characteristics of the comic may help to clarify the meaning of comedy.

Comedy is a matter of perspective, yet it is a certain kind of perspective. What is funny depends on where you stand. A pathetic old woman may be tragic when she is viewed as a social derelict or as a lonely, disregarded person. She may appear highly amusing when she is seen as a beggar acting the role of a choosy old woman. A drunk can scarcely be called a comic character; yet from Shakespeare to the present time some of the finest comedy scenes have involved characters who are inebriated. Comedy often results because the surface view is funny when beneath the comic the scene is serious and many times tragic.

A matter of perspective and knowledge! What happens to characters on a stage may be sad to them and highly humorous to the audience because the audience sees and knows much more than the people involved in the scene. Some of the funniest scenes in drama are humorous only because the spectators are aware of situations which the characters themselves cannot possibly know. The humor of most comedies of situations comes from this possibility. The ludicrous is very often the incongruous.

Older tragedy, as we have said, needed royalty and high birth for its characters. From the beginning of drama, comedy has treated all types of characters. Certain characters have been considered too sacred or too serious to be humorously treated; yet the medieval plays indicate that even God may have a sense of humor and that the most sacred characters can be funny. The fact that Satan was so often the source of humor may be the reason why sin and vice have many times been the source of comedy. Contemporary realistic dramatists are likely to take sin and vice seriously, to treat them in a sociologically analytical fashion and to find in them theological importance. Humor often depends on the accepted status of persons and their positions in a given society. Court fools are difficult to understand today and seem too often sad and pathetic. Strangely enough, this was the condition of the court fool—he was at once a brilliant wag and often a slightly unbalanced mental case. This mixture of personality is seen in the Fool in King Lear, a very comic and yet tragic figure.

To poke fun at anything is to criticize it. The line between comedy and satire is often difficult to see. People laugh at satire which holds up to ridicule and derision individual or social follies or shortcomings. When the ridicule is broad and obvious satire becomes burlesque. Satire is used to intensify incongruities, usually with an intent to provoke change for the better. Vice can be exposed and discredited through satire. When something is burlesqued it is so exaggerated that it is likely to be less severely criticized—in fact burlesque is less cruel, less trenchant than satire. Aristophanes, Shakespeare, Molière, Gay, Gilbert and Sullivan, Wilde, and Shaw are the authors of some of the world's great comedies, and they are the greatest of satirists.

Humor gives new perspective and thus presents fresh points of view. The humorous scenes in Shakespeare's *Henry IV* show Prince Hal and Falstaff with their disreputable friends. Hal in these scenes is an entirely different person from the man who meets Hotspur in battle or his father in the king's chamber. The humor fills out an all-around portrait and makes Hal one of the most intriguing characters in all Shakespeare. Hamlet with the gravediggers takes on new dimensions of tragic importance because of this comic interlude.

Divisions of comedy into high and low comedy, sentimental comedy, and comedies of manners and of character are not important except as these names indicate the special comic emphasis. A study of Molière, probably the greatest writer of comedy, reveals all types of the comic form.

Farce is comedy which treats improbable and impossible situations as if they were probable and possible. Farce is laughed at because it is improbable, and yet it is presented as if it could actually happen. It becomes hilarious because the audience knows its absurdity and yet enjoys seeing it presented.

Studies of contemporary comedy indicate that dramatists like Ionesco and Adamov are humorous because of the devastating satire which underlies the surface situation. This is humor of a high quality. Unfortunately, most humor today is on a lower level. It is obvious and often insulting to the intelligence. Where it is found, it may take its measure from the cartoon or comic strip. It is broad and lacks subtlety. A culture may be characterized by its humor. Drama from 1890 to the First World War had many excellent writers of comedy. Certainly, the comedies of Henry Arthur Jones, Arthur Wing Pinero, Oscar

Wilde, George Bernard Shaw, the early Noël Coward, and John van Druten are some of the best in English literature. Comedy declined after the Second World War as it became an escape from the tragic realities of life. It has never regained its status in the theater.

The lack of humor in religious drama is one of its most serious deficiencies. A good sense of humor is an adult accomplishment. It indicates a security that is without fear of ridicule. Humor humanizes and changes —and it is necessary in a sane life. It is a catharsis that religion and the church need.

Melodrama

The play in which the story dominates is called a melodrama. Character is subservient to story. What happens, "how the story comes out," is all-important. Unfortunately, the form has been identified with a type of play popular in the nineteenth century—the sentimental, over emotionalized, unrealistic drama found in *Uncle Tom's Cabin*, *The Girl of the Golden West*, and *Ten Nights in a Bar Room*. For the most part melodrama has been taken over today by movies and television because these media can tell a story with greater detail and with better facilities. The mass-communications media cater to the tastes of the public because they "who live to please must please to live." Soap operas and wild-west stories which once belonged to the theater now have found a better home.

Melodrama is also characterized by action; slowing down kills it. The form of drama which we now call melodrama comes from the plays of a century ago that used music to arouse the emotions. Music has disappeared, for the most part, but the adventure and the thrills are still characteristic of the melodramatic play. Detailed characterization impedes the story and, therefore, is not wanted. Type characters are easily recognizable and speed the action. Episode follows on episode, and pace is all important.

What must be emphasized again is that most plays embody several types of dramatic treatment. Shakespeare's tragedies contain comedy scenes which only heighten the dramatic impact. Many plays have elements of melodrama, so that character is subservient to plot. It is important only to recognize the great variety of forms, to appreciate the merging of forms in one play, and to enjoy the way drama has used all these forms in the involvement of face-to-face relationships.

Notes

[1] For a detailed analysis of Greek tragedy see Chapter I, Francis Fergusson, *The Idea of a Theatre* (Garden City, N. Y.: Doubleday & Company, Inc., 1953). In this book Professor Fergusson discusses the tragic rhythm of action, the actor and the theater of reason, the actor and the theater of passion, and the analogy of action, using *Oedipus Rex, Bérénice, Tristan and Isolde,* and *Hamlet* as examples of these forms of action. Various critical writings on tragedy are excellently condensed in Barret H. Clark, *European Theories of the Drama* (New York: Crown Publishers, Inc., 1947).

The best discussion of modern tragedy is found in John Gassner, *Theatre at the Cross-roads* (New York: Holt, Rinehart & Winston, Inc., 1960). See especially Chapter V, Parts I and II.

[2] James H. Clay, "A New Theory of Tragedy," *The American Educational Theatre Journal,* VIII, n. 4 (December, 1956), 296-97.

[3] From the book review section of the *New York Times* (December 16, 1945). Used by permission.

[4] Act II, scene 1. Used by permission of Random House.

Chapter III

TYPES OF DRAMATIC EXPRESSION:
FORMAL DRAMA

A. The Formal Play

FROM THE GREAT GREEK CLASSICAL PERIOD TO THE PRESENT TIME THE dramatic form has been known as a "play." Significantly enough, a play is a form that has grown and changed throughout the history of drama. It is always a representation of life—always life seen through the imagination of the writer. A play differs from all other art forms in that it is an action using characters in a situation which begins at a certain time and continues until the situation undertaken leads to another or is completed so that further action is impossible. A play is action at a particular time of tension in the lives of the characters. The action continues until the tension is resolved—until the specific tension or tensions for the time being are released.

Tensions may arise so that the outward acting of the play is largely taken up with the internal struggle in a man as he makes a choice between a constructive or a destructive action. It may be an action that consists of a struggle with conscience or with whatever a man conceives as his god. For the Greeks the tension was often between the gods and man or between man's fate and his own will. Medieval drama developed plays on biblical themes, using the story of the fall of man, the sacrifice of Isaac, the sufferings of Job, the birth of Jesus and its meaning in terms of the ultimate revelations of God and the redemption of man, and the events of the Passion of Jesus. All of these were used because the tensions between constructive and destructive forces were evident and capable of being put into action.

A play may be founded on real situations, but, as we have suggested, it is more than reality itself. The dramatist takes the situation he wishes to treat, cuts away all unnecessary material and presents the action through a scene or a series of scenes in which the characters act by means of physical movement and speech. The only physical movement that can be shown must be within the confines of the playing area—a room, a street, a place in a road, or some location, real or imaginary. The action is circumscribed by the limitations of the space and the verisimilitude of the movement as it might be in real life. The action of a play usually has a coherence in that it must begin, rise to some kind of climax, and then resolve itself in the denouement of the story. To be most effective, it must be designed to be interesting, utilitarian, and graceful. The performance of a play has always been a visual thing. It is what the audience sees. For this reason the playing space must be lighted to enable the spectators to see the action and to transmit the necessary dramatic information about the scene—the time of day, the mood of the play.

The formal play is intended to be produced before an audience that not only sees but also participates vicariously in the action. The dramatist labors for others as well as for himself. A work of art, says Ernest Grosse, presupposes a public just as much at it does an artist. "It seems safe to say that no art form would have come into existence if it were not for the hope of an audience, real or imaginary." [1] A play is always to be judged by its technical excellence, by the way in which, through action and dialogue, it presents the situation and holds the interest of the spectator and involves him in the action.

By being involved in the action, the audience, it is understood, will feel the effect of participation or "empathy." Empathy has been defined as *Einfühlung*, a feeling into, when one's own personality is merged and fused into that of some external thing. When one has sympathy for something, he is feeling *for*; when he has empathy, he is feeling *with* —he has the sense of being merged in the object or emotional experience.

Formal drama calls for a finished performance. This is discussed in other parts of the book. What is necessary to insist upon here is that the adjective "finished" characterizes the quality of the performance. Obviously no production in its first performance is ever finished. One could wish that any play carefully and sincerely produced might have more than one performance so that actors could grow in their roles, and the ensemble playing could take on the unity that is characteristic of the truly finished performance.

Too often plays done by amateurs are presented before the cast has learned its lines or before the actors, because they have been occupied with memorizing lines, have a sense of their characters. Too often production problems hinder a finished performance. The costumes have been completed just in time to wear for a dress rehearsal, yet all actors know that historic costumes may be strange and unwieldy when they have not been lived in. Lights may also cause confusion when actors find themselves in the places where the blocking of the action has been rehearsed but where lighting has not been prepared for. The actor finds himself in the dark and moves not out of necessity for the meaning of the play but out of the necessity to have his face seen.

A finished play is arrived at by a process that can be mapped out as definitely as an itinerary of a trip. In the chapter "The Play Comes Alive" a rehearsal and production schedule is given. Productions of formal plays will take longer, and less concentrated work can be done. Rehearsals will have to be worked in and around all kinds of activities. The director knows that in the weeks before the performance much time will be needed, and unless the actors and production crews can manage to give this time formal drama to be acted before an audience must not be undertaken. Dramatic activities which take less time, play-readings and role-playing, should be substituted. There is no shortcut to good performances, just as there is no shortcut to any other artistic endeavor.

B. The Pageant

Religious drama has often been condemned because it brings to mind the old church pageant which was usually given at Christmas time, on children's day, or on whatever occasion called for the participation of the whole church school. When these ill-conceived performances were derisively called "nightgown nightmares" they were aptly named. Usually the participants were either too embarrassed to want to be associated with them or enjoyed them at the expense of the serious purpose of the activity. Many of us remember some of the most humorous episodes of our youth in relation to the church pageant.

Pageants, however, have played a major role in the history of drama from the Roman era to the present. The form has been used to celebrate major events in history as well as events in the lives of people who have shaped our civilization. Most of the great Passion plays are pageants. Celebrations of Christmas and Easter can probably be most effective as pageants.

The form calls for expansive techniques, with effects which are designed to impress. Color, movement, and music have been the chief characteristics of the pageant. Its effects are scaled to larger areas than that of the formal play. At best, because of its usual size, it shows characters in situations but allows for little development of the character in the course of the action. Like Greek drama, and for the same reason, it uses both singing and speaking choruses. It usually relies on a narrator or interlocuter to weave the story together and give it unity. It cannot have much of a plot because it must rely on episodic rather than unified, well-knit action. It causes one to wonder, to be astonished, and to be excited by its effects. It is a display rather than a development of an idea or story. It impresses rather than convinces. Its glory is still seen in the opening pageants of the circus which may portray the Cinderella story or the *Wizard of Oz*. The revival of outdoor pageants in North Carolina, Tennessee, Virginia, and Kentucky has been one of the major events in contemporary theater. *The Lost Colony, Unto These Hills, The Common Glory, Wilderness Road,* and *Horn in the West* are recent examples of the historical pageant.

The decline of the pageant is due to the growth of the motion picture and its facility to present great numbers of scenes involving many people on wide screens with tremendous effects. This tends to dwarf any attempt to present a pageant as a "live" show. Thousands of people in gorgeous costumes and innumerable scenes with striking theatrical effects are now characteristic of the big feature films which have been associated with the names of D. W. Griffith and Cecil B. DeMille. What a far cry this is from the medieval mystery plays performed in the city square! These were called pageants, and the wagons on which they were performed were called pageant-wagons, their name being derived from the idea that they were movable scaffolds or stages.

Pageants have always been associated with celebrations. Today when a church wishes to celebrate some anniversary, it is likely that a historical pageant will be the first suggestion. Some highly liturgical churches use pageant techniques to celebrate great feast days of the church year. The Greek Orthodox Church employs pageant techniques on

Easter eve with processionals and hosannas sung when the tomb, represented by a room at the back of the altar, is found empty. In liturgical churches the blessing of the palms on Palm Sunday is a beautiful and meaningful spectacle.

The Church needs to rediscover ways to celebrate the great events of her history and the significant days of her calendar. What techniques will be evolved with mass-media communications remain to be seen. Until these techniques are perfected, ways of celebration by music, procession, dance, and speech should be experimented with. The Church must find her own pageant techniques and learn again the value of this form of celebration.

C. The Masque

The masque in the sixteenth century was purely a form of entertainment. It came into England as an imitation of the older Italian pageants. Royalty used the masque as a form of private entertainment until it became so elaborate it was used publicly. Allegory or mythology furnished much of the subject matter. Ben Jonson, the Elizabethan dramatist, was certainly one of the foremost writers of masques, although many of the Jacobean writers, including John Milton, tried their hands at masques. Milton's *Comus* is an excellent example of a later development of the form. Costume designs and plans for machinery and scenery are extant, so that a good idea of the techniques can be understood today. The masque is a small pageant, less episodic, and much more highly developed in subtle artistic effects that appeal to smaller and more sophisticated audiences. Someday perhaps the Church will celebrate important days and other events of the church year with a new kind of masque.

D. The Mime and Pantomime

Mimicry or miming has been generic to the peoples of the world. The word "mime" comes from the Latin word derived from the Greek verb meaning "to imitate." On the Roman stage it had a farcical or low comedy use, but it was a favorite form of entertainment. Augustus on his death bed is supposed to have asked his friends whether he had played well the mime of life. Mime is pure dramatic action. Language has been called the extension of gesture because action does speak more definitely even if not more loudly than words. Contemporary amateur actors often concentrate on the memorization of words when the words really should be the extension of something that is felt and is expressed in action.

The story material of the *mimus* was usually built on stock characters who were drawn in bold characteristics by the actors. No words were used in the later mimes, so that today we associate the word with actors who use facial movement and gestures as their means of communication. Experiments have been made in the use of miming in situations where people cannot understand the spoken language of the actor. Understanding subtle miming requires great concentration on the part of the spectators, as faces of actors must be seen and their smallest expression must be appreciated. When it is effectively used it is one of the greatest arts. At his best, Charles Chaplin was a master of mime, and there are great artists in the French theater who use only movement and facial expression in their performance. This has been vividly illustrated by the greatest of all mimes today, Marcel Marceau.

Children use mimicry before they use words. Many leaders in creative dramatics with children insist that the children mimic the action before they use words. Teachers of acting are likely to begin acting lessons by the use of pantomime. In the school of the Moscow Art Theater eurythmics and pantomime are the beginning studies.

Pantomime is fun for groups who wish to test their skills in demonstrating emotions such as joy, fear, anger, confusion, apprehension, deception, or affection. The capacity to express these in action is the beginning technique of the still greater accomplishment of adding words to the action and fulfilling the art of the actor.

E. The Play-reading and the Walking Rehearsal

Great plays are literature as well as theater. Furthermore, the moment a play comes alive before an audience is a brief one. After the performance, the moment is gone forever. In many cases, however, the text of the play is ours to read. Part of the value of the play remains for us to enjoy by reading.

Many of the great plays of the world, both ancient and modern, are too difficult for amateur production. Where can they be seen? Kenneth Thorpe Rowe has rendered a singular service by telling us that we can have a theater in our heads. By this, Rowe means that we can read plays, imagining them as acted before us. His book, *A Theater in Your Head,* is an admirable exposition of the essential principles that need to be known about production as well as about the technical structure of the play.[2] This book should be used as a guide for both private and group play-readings.

Plays are satisfying reading in that they can be read at one sitting. The world of the theater is available for us in easily accessible books. The publishing of current plays in America is an event of the last fifty years. In the early part of this century few contemporary plays were printed until they had proved themselves enduring classics. Now groups can have admirable libraries of paperback editions available to everyone. Ignorance of the background of drama and the lack of understanding of plays that can come only from reading need no longer be a problem. An extensive list of plays for reading is given in the Appendix. Many of these are in inexpensive editions.

Play-readings are valuable for giving a group familiarity with dramatic technique or with the history of the drama and the dramatic forms such as tragedy, comedy, et cetera. A play-reading can be held every month for a group that may not be able to produce more than one or two major productions a year. One thinks immediately of many plays that are not likely to be produced by a church group because they are too difficult. Reading these plays will make them familiar and will give the group more knowledge of drama than any number of lectures or discussions.

Many suggestions have been given to make play-readings effective. Readers may sit on one side of a table, or they may be seated on stools before music racks on which the script is placed. Solid racks are necessary so that scripts can be handled effortlessly. When the actors enter and leave the scene, care must be taken that their entrances and exits do not distract from the reading. Most directors of successful readings insist that all the readers be in sight, merely indicating by some physical posture when they are "on." Actors actually engaged in a scene may lean forward while reading. When they are out of the scene they may lean back as if unconcerned. If the director wishes, the persons in a scene may rise to read, returning to their chairs or stools when they are not in the scene. The use of music stands for this type of reading is felicitous because it gives the idea of a concert rather than a play. A walking rehearsal is a reading with scripts that includes as much of the action as possible.

Platforms effectively lighted by spots are good for short scenes when the play contains a number of these and the action must continue from one scene to another. A narrator is often necessary, particularly if the play has been cut for reading or if the stage directions are necessary to the understanding of the dialogue, but under no circumstances should stage directions be read. A narrator may give the setting and tell what must be known of the staging. The actual movement and action are up to the reader to indicate by his voice and by the timing of the lines.

Hand props should be avoided in play-readings, as it is most difficult to handle properties along with the script. A subtle suggestion of costume can be effective in the use of a shawl, cloak, coat, or hat. This must be done with judgment and skill so that there is no ludicrous situation or foolishness on the part of the readers.

Play-readings may be used for group discussions or for testing out plays that are suggested for production. They furnish a good way to let an entire group know the play. If the group is large enough these play-reading casts can give readings of the plays that have been selected as possible production scripts. Hearing them read, the group will be more intelligent about selecting one of them. Likewise, a director can hear the entire group read and can make judgments about individual abilities.

Many "plays with a purpose," particularly scripts produced by the United Nations, UNESCO, the Society of Friends, or the Anti-Defamation League of B'nai B'rith are not strong as dramatic writing; yet these plays, as well as those published by the Friendship Press and the National Association of Mental Health, are good for reading and discussion. Their presentation of a "cause" through a dramatic situation will compel almost any group to discuss the material presented. Thus, as informal drama they are valid and have a place in the church program.

How to Prepare and Present Play-readings and Walking Rehearsals

(Suggestions used by the Religious Drama Workshop of the National Council of Churches at Green Lake, Wisconsin)

I. Advantages
   A. A play-reading or walking rehearsal needs only two or three rehearsals; actors do not have to memorize lines

B. A play-reading or walking rehearsal does not need scenery, costumes, properties, or lights; little experience involved
C. A play-reading or walking rehearsal does not involve royalty if outside audience is not invited to attend
D. More plays and types of dramatic experience can be presented to the group

II. Requirements
  A. An adequate number of scripts
    1. One for every two persons in a play-reading (preferably one for each reader)
    2. One for each person in a walking rehearsal
  B. An adequate number of rehearsals
    1. Two rehearsals for a play-reading
    2. Three or preferably four rehearsals for a walking rehearsal
    3. Rehearsals should be an hour or an hour and a half long for a one-act play; two and a half hours for a longer play
  C. A supervisor or director
    1. An adult or responsible young person who will supervise the rehearsal
      a. Preferably a person with drama training
      b. A person who will help the actors interpret their characters with thought and feeling
      c. A person who commands the respect and co-operation of the group and takes the work seriously
  D. An adequate place to rehearse and perform
    1. For the first rehearsal there must be a place where actors can be
      a. Physically comfortable
      b. Free from interruption
      c. Accessible to informality and discussion
    2. The second and last rehearsals must be in a place that is
      a. Preferably the place where the reading or walking rehearsal will be held or a room that approximates the place of performance so that actors can check.
        (1) Volume—whether they are too loud in the more vigorous scenes or too soft in the quiet scenes
        (2) Diction—whether the words of the actors are clear and understood
      b. A place where the actor's face and body can be seen
        (1) A raised platform is preferable but not absolutely

necessary; the end or middle of a room is adequate; the audience's chairs may be staggered to increase visibility
(2) Adequate number of chairs

III. How to choose actors
  A. Everyone who wishes should have a chance to read throughout a year's time
  B. The supervisor or director, or the group may choose the people; they should be chosen for the following reasons
    1. They will take rehearsals seriously
    2. They read well
    3. They are "cast" so that they
      a. Vocally sound like the character
      b. Are not physically too different from the part
      c. Have insight and understanding of the part
      d. Will not become too inhibited before an audience
      e. Will co-operate and "act" with the other members of the cast

IV. Things that must be clear to the audience
  A. A narrator—or an actor—should describe the following things at the opening of the performance and between scenes (if there is a shift of locale and time)
    1. Place—a vivid description sets the mood; all opening actor's lines that mention place or setting should be clear and read in the proper mood; all entrances, exits, and vital properties should be mentioned by the narrator or clearly "pointed" in lines or pantomime
    2. Time—as with place should be established through narration or lines
    3. Characters and their relation to each other—most of this will be in lines, but at times may be introduced at the beginning although never during the middle of a performance
      a. This may be helped by
        (1) Important characters sit in the middle of the seating arrangement; lesser ones on the outside
        (2) Actors moving, rising, or sitting on the important lines sit beside each other
        (3) Actors should face each other when reading; bow head and shoulders and look away when not sharing the scene with other actors

b. In a walking rehearsal this may be helped by
   (1) Important actors say important lines in the most emphatic position—not blocked from the audience's view by each other
   (2) The actors moving, rising, or sitting on important lines
   (3) Actors looking at each other as much as possible, listening to each other when they are not speaking
   (4) Actors not shifting or moving while others talking
   (5) Actors not getting too crowded
   (6) Actors standing out of view of audience when they are not in the scene or "on stage"

B. When the play ends
   1. Actors may stand still a moment after closing lines; then leave in character

V. Rehearsal procedure; copies of plays have been ordered well ahead of time; rehearsals should get under way two weeks prior to the performance; rehearsals should be close enough together so that actors do not forget—one week is a good time span.
  A. First rehearsal
    1. Everyone reads the play through without interruption except to ask questions about pronunciation of words and names; strike out all printed stage directions; if a walking rehearsal, determine movements
    2. Everyone discusses the meaning of the play; questions about the background of the play; work on characterization
    3. Read through the play stopping to discuss and make suggestions about character—work for understanding and feeling the part; go through movements if a walking rehearsal
    4. If there is time read the play straight through again
  B. Second rehearsal
    1. Read straight through watching for
     a. Volume
     b. Articulation and enunciation
    2. Pick up lines quickly so there isn't too much time between lines, unless this is necessary and called for—don't let the reading drag
  C. Performance
    1. Go on and off stage, platform, or to seating arrangement in character

    2. Actor never looks at audience when reading or not reading (unless he is the narrator or the part calls for looking at the audience)

Notes

[1] Herbert Sidney Langfeld, *The Aesthetic Attitude* (New York: Harcourt, Brace and Company, 1920), p. 268.

[2] New York: Funk & Wagnalls Company, 1960. See especially Chapter 9, "Through Literature to Meaning," and Chapter 11, "Principles of Evaluation."

Chapter IV

TYPES OF DRAMATIC EXPRESSION: INFORMAL DRAMA

A. Creative Dramatics for Children

"ALL WORK AND NO PLAY MAKES JACK A DULL BOY" IS A TRUTH THAT IS now being revived in educational circles, but for reasons which our ancestors who first coined the phrase would never have used. The play theory has been broadened into a life theory, so that books are now appearing with the theses that play is the natural employment of man and that work is merely play taken too seriously. Whatever this theory of play may mean for philosophers and psychologists, it has great significance for the educator and particularly the religious educator.

To play a life situation, whether it is ancient classical lore, biblical story, or contemporary problem is to put it into action. For children this is a most natural way to express ideas. Words gain meaning as they are lived and experience gives them importance. Actions do speak louder than words for children, and they speak a language that is understandable. Young imaginations visualize a story as it is being told; to suggest that it be put into action is merely to suggest to them that it be expressed—that it be made real.

We do not need to be reminded that a child begins life by discovering his body and playing with it. He continues to play with himself and for himself until the older person intrudes with his world that is consumed with work, so that play becomes a duty and is made a requisite of health and well-being. Child's play is all consuming and all important. It is a living process. When it reaches the stage where persons other than the child are involved, he plays with them, taking them into his world that is played real. Only when others come into watch the play does the child shift his attention from play for itself to play for others.

When this happens the child plays for others and not for the mere joy of playing.

To create an environment for playing, for putting an idea into action, and to confront the child with ideas and situations that it can make come to life in its play is the problem that faces the teacher or leader of children. Anthropologists believe that play is integral to life, that it is more than an instinct. They suggest that the curtailing of play and the changing of it in the artificial living of our day is likely to have something to do with man's unhappiness and his frustration in the midst of his hectic life. Certainly, we need to return to free play, to expressing ourselves joyfully, and to social playing where we are not organized as players and coached as to how we ought to play. Our play, like our work, has become professional.

The child can begin his understanding of life by playing. If this is a free, happy experience he can carry the pattern into his adult life. Self-consciousness may be described as a kind of absence of the play spirit. The most successful adult enjoys his work; he brings to it a play spirit. Unfortunately, we have associated irresponsibility and casualness with the concept of play. Actually the highly skilled and genuinely artistic person gives himself to his work with the abandon of play, and he enjoys his work as if it were play. This is true of the skilled surgeon and of the true artist. "In the joy of the actor lies the sense of any action" can be amended to read, "In the joy of the player."

The leader of children in religious education can use their play tendency in life to achieve the greatest possible growth. A number of years ago a delightful artist by the name of Dugald Walker was confronted with the problem of directing the activities of children at Christadora House on the lower East Side in New York City. The children were not easy to handle; many were from an environment that created delinquency and lawlessness. Furthermore, there was no money for equipment. Dugald Walker found, however, that all the children had one thing in common—a joy in playing. So he decided to play a city, allowing each child to be in his imagination what he wanted most to be in life. Thus was created the "The Invisible Village." Firemen, policemen, garbage collectors, ash men, mayors, and businessmen sprang up all over the hall in which they played. Never was there anything like this in the settlement house, and for some months the recreation problem was solved; the children played the roles they longed to be. Each child in his time played more than seven ages; he played roles in an imagined life.

When drama is played by children for themselves with their own group as the only audience, it is a creative experience that has many possibilities for religious education. When disciplined into a compact form which we call a play, it is not a complete experience until it is reacted to by an audience or congregation. Drama, then, as an art form is action reacted to. Both action and reaction are necessary to it as an art.

Creative dramatics, or drama that is played by the participants without regard to any reaction except that of those taking part, is used in elementary schools and junior-high schools throughout the country. Winifred Ward's pioneering work in Evanston, Illinois, has spread to many school systems and is now a definite part of the educational process. The use of the creative method in church schools, however, is still in the early experimental stages. The reasons for this are not difficult to understand. The time element is perhaps most serious. To tell a story or create one and to have the children dramatize it and give it takes more time than the usual short period of a church-school class. The extended class period can help solve the problem of time. Very brief episodes can be done in an extended period and with some difficulty recalled and re-created another time.

Another major stumbling block to the use of the creative method is the lack of adequately prepared teachers. To keep a balance between control and spontaneous creative work is not easy. The teacher must know dramatic values and how they can be achieved naturally, and at the same time he must know how to allow complete freedom in the creative process. Above all, he must know the child and must be able to think and play as a child without superimposing his adult life and thinking on what he is doing. He must know what it means to have religious ideas come alive in action, and he must be able to meet the awful honesty and forthrightness of the child who wants his religion to be meaningful, natural, and related to everything else he is doing.

What the child dramatizes, makes come to life, will not be forgotten. What he learns in the application of life principles to contemporary settings will be much more lasting in value if he acts it out. This is a method that can be unique in an age of television. Creative dramatics, as well as formal drama, allows the child to experience a life situation in action. When he creates the story and brings it to life he is not likely to forget it. He is not merely looking at life, he is participating in it.

Religion, even for the little child, can come alive through this method. Difficult words and remote stories that are sometimes connected with the Bible need no longer frighten or bore him. Some things cannot be dramatized by children because they are adult concepts and experience. In an interview for the New York Times Miss Ward suggested that creative dramatics is fun. When fun comes back to the church-school classroom, enhancing the meanings of the materials in the curriculum, the time on Sunday can be anticipated with joy by children.

For younger children through the junior-high-school age, formal plays are educationally open to question unless they are skillfully directed. For this reason the creative method is suggested, building upon the play tendency in all children, guided, to be sure, until the child is old enough to understand the allurements of showing off in a formal play presented before an audience. The child, as we have said, must act for his own joy and for his fellow players until he is old enough to understand the reaction by others who are not actually participating in the creative act and who, unfortunately, in theater are known as audience.

There is still little written on the use of this method in the church school. Let's Play a Story by Elizabeth Allstrom, formerly supervisor of the primary department of Riverside Church in New York City, concerns story-playing for the primary and junior departments of the church school. The new revised edition of Miss Ward's definitive book Playmaking with Children has a chapter on the use of creative dramatics in the church. The principles set forth in this book are to be applied to the teaching methods in the church. The Lake Forest Workshop on religious drama and others like it throughout the country have included courses in the creative method, and many colleges and universities offer creative dramatics.

Miss Ward has condensed her definitions and techniques in the following outline. Teachers who are taking seriously the use of the creative method will need to consult the books listed at the end of this chapter. The techniques of creative dramatics should be used only by persons who understand them. After carefully studying this outline and following its suggestions, they may be successful in simple experiments, but in order to guide children with any degree of skill they will need to read further and, if possible, take a course in creative dramatics.

What is creative dramatics?

It is any type of drama created by children and played with spontaneous action and dialogue. It begins with dramatic play-living in which little children play out experiences they have had and "try on" the characters of the people around them. Under the guidance of an adult, older children in church or vacation schools plan plays or worship services based on ideas, experiences, or stories, leaving the specific action and dialogue to the individual players.

This is a different aspect of drama from the memorized, directed, rehearsed drama designed for the entertainment of an audience. It develops from the ideas of the children. Because it is improvised, it is never twice the same but is developed further each time it is played.

It influences the personal development of the children who participate by giving them:

A constructive use for their creative imagination.

Experience in working together in situations which strongly motivate co-operation.

Sensitivity to the thoughts and feelings of others which is the basis of understanding.

Controlled emotional release through playing all kinds of characters.

A heightened appreciation of the material studied.

Leadership training by way of thinking on their feet and expressing their ideas fearlessly.

It has the power to bring alive for children dramatic stories in the Bible and other literature. Also it can help them to see both sides of current problems through role-playing.

What material is good for creative plays?

Dramatic play might begin with an idea; the beginning of things, i.e., spring, homes, time, happiness, how God cares for his world.

If it is a story, it should have a central idea which is meaningful to the modern child. It should have emotional appeal, involve decisions, and offer opportunity for plenty of action. Only literature of good quality should ever be used. (Good examples of Bible stories which have these qualifications are The Good Samaritan, Joseph, and the incident in which David spares Saul's life in the cave.)

How may creative dramatics be introduced?

Before beginning any creative activity there must be a friendly, relaxed, confident feeling in the group set by the leader. Without this there can be no creative drama.

For primary children:
1. Dramatic play—the make-believe in which children learn much about themselves and others as:
   A. Playing on things constructed from blocks: Houses, boats, planes, et cetera.
   B. Playing out situations in preparation for real experiences, as: Greeting visitors, welcoming new members to the class, introducing parents.
   C. Playing out ideas of such things as love: The mother bird's care of her young, a human parent caring for a baby, God's care of nature—the snow, rain, seedlings growing up and blossoming.
2. Rhythms with music or percussion instruments. An accompanist who can improvise on the piano, one who is sensitive to the ideas of the children, is highly valuable in creative dramatics by setting a mood for their playing and guiding their dramatic rhythms. Without such an accompaniment, the leader can use drums, bells, or other percussion instruments. Records, although less satisfactory, are available for almost any activity. The RCA Victor Record Library for Elementary Schools, especially those called "Rhythmic Activities and Basic Rhythm Programs," are useful.
3. The sharpening of sense awareness, important for drama, to say nothing of its significance in life itself.
   A. The leader calls to the children's notice the beauty of colors and combinations of colors—including, perhaps, stained-glass windows if there are beautiful ones in the church—sounds which are pleasing and those which are not, objects which are interesting to the touch, flowers which are fragrant, and foods that appeal to the taste.
   B. Such questions may be asked as: "What does the color yellow make you think of?" "What is the most beautiful thing you ever saw?" "And heard?"
4. Dramatizing very simple stories, such as "Why the Evergreen Trees Keep Their Leaves in Winter" and "The Little Pink Rose." (In

Stories to Dramatize, edited by Winifred Ward.) Very few Bible stories are suitable for dramatization by primary children.

For older children: (VACATION SCHOOL)

1. Pantomimes of activities as preliminary to story dramatization:
    - A. Something you especially like to do—the others guess what it is.
    - B. Activities at camp or at a picnic.
    - C. Exploring a cave.
    - D. Searching for something. After looking in many places, find it. Show by your actions where you are, how urgent the search is, what it is that you find.
2. Characterization. (*Always* from the inside out!)
    - A. Be some definite person who finds a purse. What do you think? What do you do?
    - B. Enter and sit on a chair by a table as if you were a prim old aunt who has come to spend the day and knit. Or as a boy who is afraid he is going to be scolded. Or as an old person with rheumatism.
    - C. Be the Witch in "Hansel and Gretel."
    - D. Be the Egyptian princess when her handmaidens find the baby, Moses.

How does one guide a group into dramatizing a story?

1. The leader sets the mood for specific material by:
    - A. Capitalizing on the feeling of the group induced by the season, a holiday, or a recent experience.
    - B. Arousing interest by a picture, music, an experience, or a question.
2. Presents story with enthusiasm. Before the children can create from it the story must reach inside.

An example of procedure in creating a play from a story: FOR JUNIORS (CHURCH OR VACATION SCHOOL)

The leader may introduce the idea of good neighbors. "What do we mean when we say a person is a good neighbor?" Children discuss this in terms of their own experience.

One time when Jesus said, "Thou shalt love thy neighbor as thyself," and a man asked, "Who is my neighbor?" Jesus told the parable of the good Samaritan. The leader tells the story in his own words, making it very alive and understandable to the children. He has informed himself concerning the geography of the country, its dangers, the customs, and the feeling between Jews and Samaritans. He relates it to the children's experience in some way, such as: "Now it was only twenty miles from Jerusalem to Jericho, and today we wouldn't think that was much of a trip, would we? We'd go in a car or on the train. But in those days there were no cars and no trains. When people traveled, they either walked or rode on donkeys.

"This man had no donkey, so he was going to walk the twenty miles, starting out early in the morning with his bundle of lunch and his stout stick, expecting to reach Jericho that evening."

After telling the story as vividly and effectively as possible, the leader might say, "When Jesus had finished the story, then many knew the answer to his question, 'Who is my neighbor?' Do you?"

In the ensuing discussion, the leader might ask, "If you had been traveling along this road and had seen this wounded man, why might you have hurried past without helping him?"

Various answers will doubtless include, "I might be afraid the robbers were still around," or "He was a horrible sight and I wouldn't want to touch him." "I might be afraid people would think I had beaten him."

"Let's all of us be passersby in order to get the feel of people who for one reason or another do not stop to help him."

With some groups of children, it is better at first to use a coat to spread down for the wounded man so that there will be less chance of self-consciousness. Each one imagines and tries to show how he feels when he sees the beaten man. Perhaps one will pause as if inclined to help, another will be horrified, and still another will be fearful. Several volunteers may then try on the character of the Samaritan and his reaction to the situation.

After a discussion as to how each felt in the situation, they may play the scene with only the three passersby and the Samaritan, as well as the man who was hurt.

It is a matter of choice as to whether they begin at the beginning of the story and play it all the way through or use only the latter part of it. Sometimes children begin before the Jew leaves his home, and his wife is fearful and anxious that he wait until he can travel with others. Often, they want to start as the Jew is walking along the dangerous road, just before the robbers attack him. The Samaritan will, of course, be introduced this time, and point is made of the fact that while he has far more reason to pass by without stopping, he is the only one who does stop and help the Jew. It is always better to play a story in short units at first, putting it together afterwards.

The children often do the first playing in pantomime, adding words later. After each group plays the scene, there is an evaluation, not only by those who were not playing but by the players also. Unless the children make all the points which should be made, the leader should by all means ask questions which will cause the group to think about what was real and sincere, and what they can suggest that the scene needs.

Give the children freedom in playing.

Choosing the casts: Who would like to be the Samaritan? (The robbers will be the choice of some of the boys, and it may be the means of making dramatization fun for them.) Try to combine in each cast one or two of the freer, more imaginative children with others who are shy or less imaginative. Every player should have a feeling of achievement each time he makes a sincere effort. As often as possible, let many children play at once.

If any child is burlesquing a character or in any way spoiling the sincerity of a scene never allow the scene to go on. Without taking the child to task, call the children together and talk with them about the need for staying in character from beginning to end. That is one of "the rules of the game."

Guide them in evaluation.

Allow no negative comments at first. Instead, ask a question such as: What did you like? Or, what new ideas were added? Later ask, How can we give this scene more meaning? If the group is made up of juniors or intermediates detailed evaluation such as the following should be used:

1. Was the story clear? Was it real?

2. Were the players thinking and feeling like the characters in the story?

3. Was there good teamwork? Was everyone in the story all the time? Did each react to the others in the scene?

4. Was the action true to the story?

5. Was the dialogue true to the characters?

6. Did they make the meaning clear?

Then ask, How can we make it better? After the children have had a chance to tell how the scene can be improved, another cast is chosen —from volunteers always—and the scene is developed further. After each scene has been worked out as well as the group can do it, the whole story is put together.

Throughout the whole process in creative dramatics the leader guides the children by asking skillful questions to stir their thinking. There is little talk by the leader after the material is presented and the children are never directed or told what to say. Above all, each child is encouraged to contribute what he can and is given credit for every sincere effort.

These books will be of direct help to the teacher or leader:

Allstrom, Elizabeth. *Let's Play a Story*. New York: Friendship Press, 1957.

Brown, Jeanette Perkins. *The Storyteller in Religious Education*. Boston: Pilgrim Press, 1951.

Siks, Geraldine B. *Creative Dramatics: An Art for Children*. New York: Harper & Brothers, 1958.

Ward, Winifred. *Playmaking with Children*. Revised edition. New York: Appleton-Century-Crofts, Inc., 1957.

————, editor. *Stories to Dramatize*. Anchorage, Ky.: Children's Theatre Press, 1952.

Role-Playing for Adults[1]

Role-playing is a form of dramatic play, which, unlike creative dramatics, requires reaction from players and audience. In this form of activity people spontaneously act out problems of human relations and analyze the enactment. It is as old as certain kinds of charades in which often there is role-playing, and it is as new in its application as the forms to which it is most closely allied—sociodrama and psychodrama. Both of these newer forms require not only players but an audience which helps the players interpret their roles. Sociodrama may be defined as a form of role-playing which portrays interactions of people with other individuals or groups as carriers of some specified cultural role such as supervisor, leader, mother, father, employee, et cetera. The situation always involves more than one person and deals with problems a majority of the group faces in their lives.

Psychodrama is concerned with the unique problems of one indi-

vidual and forms release for these problems built up in the personalized
world of the actor. *It is a form of dramatic expression which should not
be experimented with except under the guidance of a therapist.*[2]

Role-playing, on the other hand, can be a delightful group activity.
It is primarily a discussion technique, since its purpose is to stimulate
discussion by the group which observes the technique. It is, in fact,
one of the best methods to get a group involved in the discussion of a
subject. As is true with any dramatic technique, role-playing brings a
subject to life and thus makes a given situation more real than any
description of it could be. The actors as well as the observers "live
through" the situation presented. With this emotional involvement,
the participant, both actor and observer, is able to test his knowledge
and judgment about the situation, and to have this checked by the
experience of the group. In this way, individuals may gain new skills
for dealing with problems in human relations. A contrived situation
may not apply to the specific problems faced by the group. It is only
when the group has set up the problem as one real for itself that it will
appreciate the relevance of this method in dealing with social problems.

Role-playing also allows many different attitudes and feelings to be
expressed, so that as they are objectified their validity can be tested.
In a meeting of the National Association of Foreign Student Advisors
on one of the campuses of America, a delightful afternoon was spent
showing by role-playing the right and wrong methods of dealing with
many of the problems of foreign students when they came to this
country. Students from other countries were used in the playing so
that their individual grievances, as well as the mistaken theories of some
of the advisors, were aired. What was particularly interesting was that
everyone agreed that the method made much more impressive what
needed to be known, and the discussion following each role-playing
episode was more lively than any of the discussions in the conference.
Some of the group became so involved that they decided they should
demonstrate the right methods of dealing with their problems.

How does a group go about using role-playing as a learning device?
Like most dramatic presentations, role-playing needs a director who
is responsible for all the procedural aspects involved in the process and
who helps the actors and other group members (observers) become
emotionally involved with the situation to be acted out. The director
may be the group leader or some other member who is familiar with

the role-playing process. Unlike a director in a legitimate theater production, however, whose main function is to help actors interpret already written lines and characterizations, a director of role-playing is mainly concerned with helping the actors to be spontaneous in presenting the characters they are portraying and with helping the audience-observers to analyze the situation and behaviors presented in order to increase their insights into problems and their knowledge of how to deal with them effectively.

As an educational technique role-playing involves more than the simple acting out of roles. It is made up of a series of steps, of which the actual acting is only one, and it is the director's job to see that all these steps are taken care of in every role-playing situation and that the function of each step is understood by everyone in the group. In practice, these help the group understand the significance of each of them. In brief, the steps in the role-playing process are: Defining the problem, establishing a situation, casting characters, briefing and warming up actors and observers, acting, cutting, discussing and analyzing the situation and behavior by actors and observers, and making plans for further testing of the insights gained or for practicing the new behavior implied.

Most groups will welcome a suggestion to try role-playing in their meetings, as most people like opportunities for dramatic expression and like to try new ways of bringing content into their group meetings. Some groups, however, may be hesitant about role-playing or even frightened because they do not see themselves as "actors" or because they are afraid such spontaneous expression and exploration of problems may get too close to personal anxieties and problems.

Groups which appear hesitant will quickly learn to feel at ease by starting with a simple situation which can be initiated by some problem with which the group is dealing. One member of a discussion group, for example, might be having a heated argument with another over the right of farmers to receive production subsidies. The first member insists that the second member cannot look at the problem objectively because he has a farm background and will always be in favor of anything that helps the farmers, whether or not it hurts the rest of the country. A third member of the group, or the group leader, could easily introduce role-playing as a way of helping each party to this argument get a better understanding of the other's point of view. He might suggest that each of the contenders stops the argument and portrays the other person, seeing how accurately each can represent the other's point of view. After a few minutes of this attempt to reverse roles, each person could be asked to describe how he felt in the role of the other, or if he thought he might have been oversimplifying or stereotyping the other's position. This simple but effective way of using role-playing has the advantage of needing almost no preparation. It automatically briefs and warms up the participants. After such an experience, some other uses of role-playing could be described to the group.

Generally, when role-playing is used for the first time, the situation selected should be simple enough to allow group members to discuss it profitably. It is important that group members have the experience of discovering that with the leader or director's guidance they can explore a problem, break it down into factors which may be causing it, and construct ways of meeting the problem through changing the situation or their behavior. It is also generally true that while an experienced group leader can take on the job of directing role-playing readily, an inexperienced group leader may feel too burdened to charge himself with sole responsibility as a director and may want to involve group members in this task with him.

Overpersonalization of Problems

The role-playing director can do much to help a group steer clear of psychodramatic situations and analyses by being on the alert to avoid situations and roles which lead to personal exposures or are so closely related to personal and private feelings that psychodramatic expression can hardly help. The director sets the tone for portrayals and analyses in introducing briefing and discussion by pointing out that the job of the observers is to look at the actors in terms of their roles. It should be made clear that each actor is playing a specified role in a specific situation and is merely giving his spontaneous interpretation of how such a character would be likely to respond in such a situation.

Overuse of Role-Playing

Groups which are new to role-playing as an educational technique sometimes get very interested in it and begin to use it as a cure-all. Such inappropriate overuse may lessen its effectiveness when it should be used. If role-playing is to be an effective training tool it must assume

its proper place among other educational methods in the group's repertoire. It is wise to remember that role-playing is useful in dealing with
a very distinct group of problems only—that is, problems involving
human relations. There are many other procedures which are sufficient
to meet the educational requirements of many group situations, and
sometimes it is wise to reserve role-playing only for those situations
where it is crucially required.

Finally, when role-playing is used it can be enriched and varied by
adapting variations and new forms to the basic structure. Groups that
have gained some experience with the basic technique will want to
build new or more complex structures for getting at specific problems.
Some such ideas—the use of alter-ego techniques, consultants to the
actors, et cetera—are described in the literature on role-playing, but
many groups will be able to invent these adaptations in relation to their
own specific needs. In fact, the basic role-playing technique offers one
of the best opportunities for exploiting the inventive abilities of any
group.

The design of role-playing is always dependent on the learning out-
comes desired or needed by the group. The planners must always work
with the training purpose of role-playing uppermost in mind.

There are several ways by which situations can be designed:

1. A subcommittee can plan the situation and bring it to the group.
2. The total group can make up a situation on the spot.
3. A member or the leader can suggest an actual case which illustrates
the problem. (If this method is used care must be taken to see that
the scene doesn't get clogged up in details about what really happened.)

The responsibility for defining and casting characters may be taken
by the total group or delegated to certain members. The planners must
think about what kinds of characters will have meaning for the group
and will contribute to the group's understanding of the problem. If
the director or planners are not well acquainted with the group members and do not know how they would feel about taking roles in the play
it is probably wiser to ask for volunteers or suggestions from the members
during the meeting rather than to assign parts in advance. In general,
persons should be chosen because it is thought they can carry the role
well and are not likely to be threatened or exposed by it.

Regardless of what method is used for casting, no one should ever
be asked to take a role unless he is definitely willing to do so. If an

individual plays a role under forced circumstances, he is likely to give a constricted and nonspontaneous portrayal of the role.

If a role has unfavorable characteristics, it is wise to assign it to a person who has enough status in the group or enough personal security to carry it without stress, or if the group is a new one, its leader might be asked to take this role to get things moving.

When dealing with beginners at role-playing it may be wise to start them in roles in which they feel at home and confident. Soon, however, they should also be assigned roles which will help them stretch their perceptions and insights.

If the situation is simple, it may be better to depend on oral briefing. Because spontaneity is such an important element in role-playing, over-preparation may restrict the players or even cause them to ham their roles.

No attempt should be made under any circumstances to use the briefing or warm-up process to structure what the actors are going to say or do in the action.

When the role-players have no hidden motives, they can warm up by talking among themselves about their parts, setting up the physical properties on the stage "in role," by saying, "This is our house. We have lived here forty years. This is the door, et cetera."

One of the most important responsibilities of the director is to see that everyone moves into the role-play at the same time. The mood of the play can be destroyed after the action has started if one of the actors begins to talk as himself rather than as the character he is portraying.

A common tendency is to let the scene go on too long. Generally, role-playing should be cut when:

1. Enough behavior has been exhibited so that the group can analyze the problem it has set for itself.

2. The group can project what would happen if the action were continued.

3. The players have reached an impasse because they have somehow been miscast or misbriefed.

4. There is a natural closing.

The director must always be alert to see that the discussion relates to the original problem.

Sometimes the players are asked to comment first, and sometimes the discussion is started by the observers. The advantages of the former in some situations is that it allows the players to set the tone for constructive criticism. If the players show by their own observations that they are unselfconscious because they are analyzing the characters portrayed and not themselves the observers are more likely to feel free to express their full reactions.

It is important that the observers steer clear of comments that evaluate the acting ability of the players or the convincingness of the players' interpretations of their roles. The discussion should be focused on what the play can contribute to their understanding of the problem they were trying to solve.

The observers should try to bring into the discussion what they saw and heard, rather than commenting on what should or should not have been done.

If the diagnosis of the problem opens up a whole new way of working at things the group might try a different role-playing situation to see if their generalizations hold true in more than the specific case, the leader or director might suggest readings for the group to explore the problem further, or the group may plan to have a future discussion on other aspects of the problem.

Notes

[1] The author is indebted to the Adult Education Association of the United States of America for much of the substance of this discussion. Two helpful resources are *Role-Playing Methods in the Classroom* by Mark Chessler and Robert Fox (Chicago: Science Research Associates, 1966), 86-page pamphlet; and *Creative Procedure for Adult Groups* (of which role-playing is one) by Harold D. Minor, available from Discipleship Resources, P.O. Box 840, Nashville, Tennessee 37212.

[2] Dr. J. L. Moreno has been the pioneer in the use of psychodrama. His book on psychodrama should be consulted for the explanation of its use. *Psychodrama and Sociodrama* (Boston: Beacon Press, 1946).

Part two

Chapter V

WHAT IS RELIGIOUS DRAMA?

RELIGIOUS DRAMA IS NOT A KIND OF DRAMA, IT IS A QUALITY OF DRAMA. It is produced like any other type of drama, but the quality of the production is judged both by the artistic and theatrical results as well as by a quality inherent in the process of production itself. Religious drama presupposes a standard of work that is religiously oriented. It is dramatic activity in its finest expression, since it is concerned with persons both as the characters in the play and as persons who are bringing the characters of life in the production. It is, therefore, potentially a genuinely religious activity.

Drama is not religious because it uses material that comes from religious books or from Judeo-Christian sources in the Bible. It is not religious because it dramatizes so-called religious themes. These may give religious significance to the material, but they are not its only source. Drama is truly religious when it shows meanings and purposes in life that grow from the revelation of the highest values conceivable. It seeks to relate man to the totality of his being. When these values are translated into living situations which cause conflicts with lesser meanings and purposes, then religiously effective drama may occur. When life situations are filtered through dramatic imagination they may be presented in terms of the perspective of the ultimate concerns and purposes of men or they may be presented merely as experiences in a laboratory of life. The former is likely to be the framework of religious drama, the latter that of realism which may or may not have religious meaning.

Plays may have ethical and moral values because they probe into motivations. In a very real sense the religious value of a play grows from the *motivations which drive the characters to action*. The deeper the motivation for action, the more likely it is that the play will have religious significance. This does not mean, necessarily, that the play will be a good play because of its concepts. A good play is judged by dramatic standards. The finer and sounder the subject matter, the more likely will the dramatist be able to create a good play. *Religious drama presents characters in action in situations where faith and belief are tested in lives of people at tension moments.*

The Stage Manager in the last speech in Thornton Wilder's *Our Town* looks up at the stars while he makes the observation that scholars seem to think that none of the other stars is inhabited: "Only this one," the earth, he adds by way of benediction, "is straining away, straining away all the time to make something of itself." Religious drama is *man's straining away trying to make something of himself* because he is endowed with this capacity by his creator.

Plays that bring to an audience a depth experience of conflict which is not artificial and not fantastic, with a story that is accepted because its plot and characters come out of genuine life situations and call for emotional responses that are constructive and elevating, is religious drama. By this definition many of the plays of Ibsen, Shaw, and other continental dramatists, as well as those of T. S. Eliot and Christopher Fry, have given new dimensions to the meaning of religious drama. Christian, Muslim, Hindu, or Jewish drama are specific kinds of religious drama.

Religious drama, furthermore, deals with characters, situations, and themes that are clarified by means of religion, by man's relationship with his God, with himself, and with his fellow man because of the nature and meaning of his God. It should have high seriousness of purpose whether it is comic or tragic. It derives its meaning from man's struggle to fulfill his destiny to the best of his ability. It communicates life on its deepest level.

Roderick Robertson suggests three basic areas of human experience which religious drama may treat.[1] In the first area drama deals with man's state as unrelated to God and may be called the *drama of religious alienation.* Eugene O'Neill's *Days Without End* is a play of this type. In the second area it deals with the process through which man goes in order to achieve his relationship to God and may be called the *drama of the religious experience.* Ronald Duncan's *This Way to the Tomb* belongs in this category. In the third group are dramas concerned with the person who has found a successful orientation to God, or the *drama of the religious hero*. Shaw's *Saint Joan* immediately comes to mind as an example of a play which has this kind of heroine.

The attempt to arrive at a definition of religious drama is a continuing project. Some clarification has been possible in definitions arrived at through group processes and through the research that has taken place in colleges. The Religious Drama Project of the American Educational Theatre Association framed the following definition:

Religious drama includes not only a literature but also a body of acts and skills religiously inspired and motivated. Religious drama, as literature, is based upon a centrally religious theme and has a religious impact upon its participants and witnesses. This may include experiences of worship, plays for entertainment, educational drama, and creative dramatics. It is not concerned exclusively with propaganda and/or edification. It is not limited to acts of worship and chancel drama, although it may be of these things. Religious drama is written, produced, and performed in a spirit of reverence and with concern for the enrichment of its participants, church, and community.

In a Religious Drama Workshop held at Boston University, in the summer of 1959, other suggestive definitions were formulated. Some of these are given here to show the range of thinking and the broad scope of the kind of drama called religious.

Religious drama is action involving man in the ultimate concerns of his relationship with man and God for the purpose of aiding him in his search for maturity.

Religious drama is the enactment through staged action and dialogue of human situations that convey men's concepts about ultimate reality; and the transcendence of that enactment into a relationship that involves the participants (actors and audience) with the concepts presented.

A religious drama is any drama which allows man to discover or deepen his own relationship to the ultimate, or God.

Religious drama is a peculiar attempt to communicate through involvement of writer, actors, and audience by means of psychological, physical and mental action, man's endeavor to respond with his whole being to that which is most real and most important.

Another definition contributed by Marvin Halverson pinpoints Christian drama:

Drama is an art form which has evocative and communicative power which causes one to confront the human situation—and one's self. This is true of Greek tragedy and contemporary skeptical drama. Christian drama, however, points beyond the depths of tragedy to that fulfillment of life which is seen in Jesus, the Christ. Christian drama, like corporate worship, derives its content as well as its structure from the drama of the biblical story, and particularly, the Incarnation, ministry, Passion, death and resurrection of Jesus Christ. Such drama makes men experience not only pity, fear, and catharsis, but also guilt, judgment, and the forgiveness of God which brings the "peace that passeth understanding." [2]

Christian drama mentioned in this definition has certain specific characteristics. E. Martin Browne, writing in *motive*, suggests some of them:

The most important thing of all about drama for us Christians is: *that it partakes of the nature of incarnation* . . . that the coming of God to earth as man, the Word made flesh, is the climax of all human development in all fields. . . . So we see the Incarnation as God's use of the dramatic form in human history, as God's action in human life. The word drama itself simply means "doing." [3]

The Danish dramatist Kaj Munk in a ringing declaration written for the program of the first production in 1938 of *He Sits at the Melting Pot* expresses in another way the significance of Christian drama:

The Christian God is a great God. He is so just that he cannot do with less than a God as stoker at his foundry. It is the God of hell who shovels in the coal under God's melting pot. That is why the heat is so terrific, and has to be, in order that the dross may be cleansed away. . . . Will it be cleansed away? What does mankind know? . . . Christianity robs life of none of its thrills. *It is the religion of drama.*

Preston Roberts has further illuminated the meaning of Christian drama. He suggests that Christian dramatic tragedies turn upon the theme of man's idolatry and pretension rather than upon the themes of man's suffering nobility or piteous abnormality. "They move from fate

to freedom, from defeat to victory, from doom to grace, and from tragedy to peace." [4]

A Christian tragic hero may abuse the radical freedom which is his—
he is free to respond to God, to others, to his own conscience, to forgiveness, to God's grace. The effect of the Christian play on the audience
is that of judgment and forgiveness rather than a sense of pity and terror
as in Greek plays or despair as in the modern, skeptical play. Dr. Roberts
points out that the meaning of Greek and modern plays is "despair,
virtually complete and unmitigated, whereas the meaning of a Christian
dramatic tragedy is that life and history are redeemable in principle
and are in part redeemed at certain crucial points and moments in
fact." [5]

More and more persons have come to respect the French dramatist
Henri Ghéon. In the preface to the collection of his plays, *Saint Anne
and the Gouty Rector*, the translator, Marcus S. Goldman, suggests that
Ghéon sought to express his Christian faith in all his writing. He had a
sensitive, artistic conscience, but he did not believe that piety and good
intentions could make up for poor writing. He felt that his highest duty
as a dramatist was to write plays which would act well and entertain
the public. His first purpose was not to teach but "to delight." As an
artist, he regarded with horror and scorn the pious theatrical performances usually presented under ecclesiastical auspices. He referred to
them as *bondieuseries*, a word that can be translated as "goodgoderies"
but which probably ought to be translated as "goodie-goderies," the
pious, goody-goody plays he sought to run from the scene.

Ghéon used humor in all his plays. What a cleansing, revitalizing
thing it is in religious drama! The medieval writers used it, too, as we
can see in *The Second Shepherd's Play* of the Townley cycle of mystery
plays. Ghéon felt that religion, and specifically Christianity, had a place
in the theater. If an actor could be asked to take the part of a Homeric
hero or a Greek god, why should he not be asked to take the part of an
Old Testament prophet or a disciple of Jesus? Laughter can be mingled
with true piety, however, and this along with a true dramatic sense, was
Ghéon's great contribution to religious drama. His plays are some of the
best we have.

Morality is not only doing right; it is discovering what is right. Moral
problems are those arising out of sincerity and conscience, not those created out of living according to moral law. Drama helps us to discover

what is right by showing us people who do the right or wrong things.

Ernest Toller, the German dramatist of the First-World-War years, reminded us that artists were not to serve the tastes of their day, but were to serve the eternal powers of life, truth, justice, joy, beauty, freedom, the mind, and the spirit. These are the subject matter of true religious drama. The Italian artist Enrico Prampolini has gone even further by insisting that the future theater will use time and space as dynamic elements to serve the function of "spiritual education."

Shelley, in the preface to The Cenci, speaks of the illuminating power of the drama when he says: "The highest moral purpose aimed at in the highest species of the drama, is the teaching of the human heart, through its sympathies, the knowledge of itself." Thus, drama in the theater can reveal the human heart to itself. It can also reveal the human heart in its leap to immortal things and "show the trace" in the lives of men.

Fräulein Schmidt in Kaj Munk's He Sits at the Melting Pot, a vivid, melodramatic play written at the height of German occupation in Denmark, says: "Then let it be play-acting, and let this be the great idea of the play—that we may be allowed to come out of our narrow selves."

The capacity of drama as it comes alive in performance to let human beings "come out of their narrow selves" is one of its most important functions. This is what is meant by perspective, by vicarious experience that drama alone can give. It can also do this by "purgation," as Aristotle called it, or by release that can be found in delight and enjoyment. It is important to understand that significant drama or religious drama is characterized by its possibilities for illuminating the private world of the spectator—illumination that allows him to come out of his narrow self. Any drama or theater that can do this will have religious value.

In drama one can walk with kings and not lose the common touch, or one can associate with individuals and groups that are not accessible even to the most cosmopolitan person. In the theater one can see history come alive and ideas take shape in human situations, and one can see revealed what never was revealed before—the inner working of the mind outwardly and the insights of the imaginative artist demonstrating themselves in human forms.

The essential religious values of any play are found first of all in the subject matter of the script. When these are communicated to the audience in performance, a dimension of religious significance is added to the theater.

In other parts of this book religious values in the total activity of producing a play will be discussed. These relate to the leadership in the group, the significance of the director, the "atmosphere" of the church as a producing center, and the effect of the play on the audience. These are all important aspects of the religious-drama experience.

Notes

[1] "Toward a Definition of Religious Drama," *The Journal of The American Educational Theatre Association*, IX, n. 2 (May, 1957), 99.

[2] Quoted from Marvin Halverson at the National Council of Churches Religious Drama Workshop, Greenlake, Wisconsin, 1955.

[3] (April, 1958), p. 10.

[4] Preston Roberts, "Christian Theory of Dramatic Tragedy," *The Journal of Religion*, XXXI, n. 1 (January, 1951), 7.

[5] *Ibid.*, p. 13.

Chapter VI

A BRIEF HISTORY OF RELIGIOUS DRAMA

ONE FINE SPRING DAY MILLIONS OF YEARS AGO ONE OF OUR LESS HOUSE-broken ancestors looked out upon the primeval forest and the unculti-vated plain. The warm sun had returned again, and he felt the sense of returning life in the world. He had learned to recognize certain plants as good to the taste. He saw these coming out of the ground that morning, and he felt instinctively glad. He knew that the sun caused the plants to grow, that rain was necessary, and that frost and cold retarded growth. Naturally, this primitive man wished that the sun would shine, that the warm rain would come, and that the plants would mature. He gave utterance to this wish, perhaps in the form of a song or an uttered petition to the unknown powers he felt were responsible for the sun and the rain and the wind.

His plea was repeated, this time with other men like himself, and the place where the plea was raised, especially if the supplication was answered, became for them a sacred place. It might have been at the top of a hill where the sky could be clearly seen. It might have been at the base of a cliff where protection from the wind and rain would have been possible. Wherever it was, it became the place of petition to the powers that be, and for the time being it was set apart for that purpose. This may have been man's first shrine. Here he uttered his first sincere petition. Here at the time of harvest, he sang his first song of thanksgiving. Here, too, he may have come when hunting was not good, when hurricanes struck, when wild animals devoured his stores of food or killed those with whom he lived. With the other men, women, and children he came to this shrine. Together they raised their petitions in songs, the rhythms of which gave them incentive to walk in a procession, and finally they delegated to certain persons duties and action that were particularly significant in the worship.

Man lived in a hostile world where survival of the physically strongest was the rule. Even at this early time he was seeking some way to under-stand the universe and to put himself more completely into harmony with it. He had learned that to defy nature was suicide. Yet he had not sufficiently learned the laws to understand how they might best be used to make for life and not for death. This long process of learning is still going on, and even after millions of years man is confronted with the struggle of life that eventuates either in tragedy or comedy, depending on the way he plays his role.

To please the powers that brought heat and moisture, we can imagine primitive man erecting a stone structure on which he placed gifts he thought the powers might like—the first fruits of his harvest or the finest specimens of his hunting. Nature was often cruel. Frosts killed the early growth and stunted the fruit, and animals filched the store of the hunting. Man was opposed by nature. To overcome this opposi-tion, he thought that more appeasement was necessary. Soon he made images of the powers of nature and gave them human form and human characteristics so that by talking with them, humoring them, bargaining with them became easier. Quite by accident he discovered that when he did certain things certain other things resulted. By this trial-and-error method he came to find the right ways of dealing with the powers and the more advantageous procedures that would guarantee his success. As he transferred human characteristics to the powers or gods, he found himself struggling with them. Their jealousy and ambition were pitted against his jealousy and ambition.

As the spring came we can conjecture that he learned to construct a little story about the return of mother nature from some hidden place where she had been held captive during the winter. He re-enacted this story as a greeting to the spring, putting it into action, performing it with his fellows at the time that was formerly given over to incantations and petitions. Everyone, including the powers of nature, he felt, liked this, and stated occasions for such action became popular. Because the acted story took more concerted effort and used more persons, co-operation was necessary. The struggle of the powers of darkness against the powers of light and life was dramatized in the story of the return of spring. Certain individuals developed abilities to perform the story more effectively and thereby gained popularity. In the course of time man set apart these favorite places where creative dramatics began to solidify into formal drama. Soon the places were to be further marked by playing spaces and by shelters against the weather. The world was to know its first play, its first theater, and its first place of worship.

Worship and drama were probably born together. The emotional expression of a petition, the emphasis upon a word, the manner of walking, the pattern of a celebration, and finally the story of the conflict between the forces of good and evil—all these were to become the dramatic elements of this primitive worship. As these "occasions" became more interesting, man created devices to appeal to larger groups. Words spoken together were easier to understand, and words sung together could raise greater emotional response from the group. Action spoke more effectively than words even at this early time, symbols carried meanings when words confused, and silence often seemed filled with emotion while noise seemed to distract.

At this early stage in primitive civilization, all dramatic expression had form; it was structured, however crude, with a beginning, a sequence in time, and an end. There was a sense of progression, of climax in every performance. Something special that was anticipated, something that differentiated it from the ordinary round of life made it a break in the customary routine. It became celebration.

The drama of native peoples was developed by the people, and the ceremonies recaptured group experiences of earlier days. Song, dance, myth, and poetry were all integrated in the performance. Masks were created by primitive graphic and plastic artists, as were costumes and other paraphernalia for the celebration.[1]

Obviously, there is no line of demarcation between primitive and civilized drama. "In beauty of physical movement, richness of costuming, effectiveness of music, impressiveness of masks, primitive drama is often superior to the drama of culture; in literary expression, subtlety of thought, mechanical equipment, and organization, the latter is obviously superior."[2]

Primitive man believed in a sympathetic magic. He was surrounded by the mysteries of nature, and as Glenn Hughes has pointed out, he lacked any adequate explanation of them. Thus the theory that imitation is a "potent act" has evolved. The act of imitation is as old as man—it is the art of acting. And acting that evoked magic was essentially a religious act because magic itself was a divine process since it was related to forces and powers greater than man.

Other essentially religious concepts occur very early in drama. Penance and sacrifice are characteristic dramatic rituals in the earliest known celebrations. The early Greeks offered the lives of virgins to their deities; later they substituted sheep and other animals. The later sacrificial, symbolic rites developed from the more primitive ones.

Primitive drama, the expression of the communal or religious life of the organic human group, the tribe, had spontaneously the unity of a pure art. There may be two hundred actors dramatically dancing the conflict of winter and spring, but all that all of them do in that drama springs from one shared fund of feelings, ideas, impulses. Unity is not imposed on them by the will of one of their number, but comes from that deep level in the spirit of each where all their spirits are one.[3]

The ancient Egyptians had a dramatic statement of the rebirth of life from the ground that is interesting to study in its relation to the concepts of Easter. The overflow of the Nile meant plenty or famine. The Nile was called Father Osiris, and the land was known as Mother Isis. The annual overflow was the embrace of Mother Isis by her spouse, during which he impregnated her with the life that was to be born during the harvest. The overflow depended upon the melting of the snow in the mountains by the moon, by the sun. The sun was Horus, less powerful than Osiris because the sun could not give life, since he shone in the desert where all was dead, while life bloomed wherever Osiris touched. Therefore they depicted in their great mysteries, the death of Osiris at the hands of the demon Drought, his entomb-ment and Mother Isis' waiting for him, Horus searching for his father and restoring him to life by his magic eye, the sun, and the happiness of Egypt as a result. This was the basis of those splendid and shadowy dramas which filled Heroditus with awe.

Glenn Hughes maintains that while the Hebrews, Egyptians, and Turks never advanced beyond "a rudimentary sort of theatrical expression," the Greeks, Hindus, Chinese, and Japanese achieved elaborate and extraordinarily effective theatrical systems. "The nontheatrical races are only cases of arrested development."[4] Certainly the Jews were not without a dramatic sense in their elaborate feasts, their ceremonials, and their symbolic national role of a chosen people. The Egyptians excelled in dancing which obviously had its dramatic significance, and the Turks were famous for shadow puppets, if not for live drama. Their lives were full of dramatic incident that still needs to be put into dramatic form.

For anyone who has lived in India drama seems a natural mode of expression. The love for ceremonials, the passion for celebration, both religious and secular, and the inherently dramatic events in the lives of most of Indian deities are generic to the Hindu way of life.

The Indian theater is supposed to have grown from the conception of Brahma, the creator, in his meditation as a means of bringing joy to all people. He inspired Bharata to write the Upageda, which is a treatise on dance, drama, and music, which forms the religious-philosophic cornerstone of the many-faceted art of the dance in India. Dance in India is three or four thousand years old, and it is so integrally bound up with drama that the two cannot be separated.

Religion is meaningful to the Hindu in a very real way through ceremonials. His interest has been fostered and kept alive through the celebrations which occur on all days and seasons set apart to pay homage to the deities. All later drama in India—seen best in the performances in villages on the birthday of Krishna or local deities—is largely re-enactment of legend or history in the form of dramatized myths. Music, dance, and pantomime belong in the Indian theater, and all are highly developed in intricate ways that baffle the Westerner but give enduring delight to the Indian. In many ways the village drama of India is similar to the medieval mystery plays. These are India's educational dramatics.

Theorists of the Hindu theater have classified many modes created by dramatic presentation; these include the exotic, the comical, the pathetic, the tragic, the heroic, the hateful, and the miraculous. They have discovered 48 types of heroes, 385 types of females, and many varieties of villains, comedians, and confidants. Contemporary student groups enjoy nothing more than the performance of both Eastern and Western drama. Remarkable, too, is the way in which dramatic interest has found an outlet in the motion picture; India now ranks among the three or four leading producers of movies in the world. Many are founded on religious myths and heroic figures, and all integrate pantomime, dance, and music into the fabric of the myth or history that constitutes the story of the play.

Only recently has the drama of other oriental countries attracted our attention. How interesting it is that in Java none of the arts exist independently of the theater! The intricately carved and beautifully painted shadow puppets have been used to evoke the spirits of ancestors. Originally each family had its own puppets; then the puppets passed to the priests and finally to professional manipulators who still remain among the most skilled artists in the world. Here again we see the secularization of the dramatic art along with the secularization of the subject matter of the plays.

When live actors were substituted for the puppets the physical movements of the puppets were imitated. Today in Jakarta one can see the ancient religiously oriented shadow puppets, as well as modern dramatic forms with live actors, and all are artistically presented with dance and music native to the performance. Theater historians are now suggesting that in the history of the Javanese theater we can see the evolution from religious ritual to secular art in a striking way. We shall also observe the same evolution in all the Western countries.

Before the Christian Era—some historians suggesting as far back as 2000 B.C.—the Chinese were developing a theatrical art. In temples and palaces religious festivals were held in which spectacle and dramatic rituals were recorded in drawings and paintings. The oldest extant specimens of Chinese dramatic literature go back only to the sixth century A.D. In the Yuan dynasty (1280-1368) at the time of the Mongol emperors, well-developed plays existed.

In ancient China, dramatic writing was placed in a category lower than poetry, philosophy, and painting. Interestingly enough, this was because drama was thought of as writing in the vernacular, somewhat more vulgar than the delicate statement of poetry. Then, too, drama was not written in classical Chinese, which is quite different from the language of conversation.

In the golden age of Chinese culture during the Ming dynasty (1368-1644)—corresponding so remarkably with the Renaissance in the Western world—dramatic literature flourished. Cycles of plays divisible by four, some reaching the length of forty-eight plays, were written. Four of these were always performed at the same time.

Chinese plays ought rightly to be called operas, for they are acted to music and are sung. The subject matter is myth and legend. To the Westerner they seem terribly verbose and slow. They are written to amuse and to instruct, with good triumphing and evil always defeated. All scenery and properties are symbolic. They leave everything to the imagination of the spectator. A table may be a mountain, and a journey of a thousand miles over rivers and mountains can be taken back and forth across the stage. The stage manager, always present, plays a singularly important role in the performance.

The Chinese drama came from ritual, and it has never lost its ritualistic character—it does not represent nor does it cope with reality. It is a unique, distinct art form.

Religious dances with masks, accompanied by chants and music, were given in the temples of Japan at a very early period, but the literary drama of Japan does not seem to have been recorded and solidified until sometime in the fourteenth century. A shogun, Yoshimitsu, enjoyed the dancing of a priest, Kwanami, and brought him to the court in 1375. Kwanami developed the art of dramatic representation and with his fellow priests arranged the first real dramas of Japan. They dealt with religious subjects, but their appeal was aesthetic because the gestures, postures, and rhythmical movements of the dancers were based on a symbolic system. This classical performance was called Nō which means drama or something done.

Nō plays using elaborate costumes and headdresses are short and often are merely efforts to establish a mood or set forth a poetic atmosphere. Buddhism dominates many of these early plays so that they are understandable best by adherents of Buddha and his many interpreters. In this sense these are truly religiously based plays, without comedy and completely unrealistic. Some critics suggest that the Nō plays are the most significant specimens of ritualistic drama in the world today.

Popular theater aimed at entertainment did not appear in Japan until two centuries after Nō was established. The doll-play and Kabuki are both famous examples of the popular theater, the former being a puppet theater where music and narration are used. Kabuki began with a religious dancer, in this case, a woman. Her dancing was soon to veer away from its religious origin and to become secular. She assumed the role of warriors and, with her Samurai husband as her composer, established what was to be called Kabuki. The interchange of sexes in the actors and the fact that less high-minded artists were attracted to this performance caused Kabuki to be shunned by respectable people. The abolition of women's companies gave older men a better chance, with families establishing their reputation as actors, and the form was gradually given status. It is still enormously popular in Japan today. The contemporary stage in Japan also includes Western styles of acting and production. Motion pictures have been highly developed, with some of our best pictures originating in Japanese studios.

Ancient Greek drama may have sprung from funeral dirges, from the celebrations of the Eleusinian mysteries, from the concept of the "year spirit," or from satyric drama. The spring season was symbolic of the spirit of rebirth and coincided with the chief worship period of Dionysus, who was also known as Bacchus, the god of wine and fertility. The ode in honor of Dionysus, expressed through song and dance, was known as the dithyramb. This may have been improvisation at first, but certainly by the sixth century B.C. it had become a regular form of literature with a chorus of fifty dancing and singing in a formal composition. In the festival in honor of Dionysus in 534 B.C., there was a contest in tragedy as the chief feature of the program.

Tragedy in this sense was an action that was serious. The satyrs, dressed as goats, give us the word tragedy which originally meant "goat song." Greek tragedy was a music drama or sacred oratorio. The place where the dithyramb took place, the theater of this event, was the place of worship for Dionysus where the only scenery was an altar. When one of the actors dressed himself as the god Dionysus and had the other performers become the god's followers, impersonation was established and acting began.[5]

The state produced the religious festival which gave birth to drama. Dancing was highly important in worship. It was genuinely a social activity co-ordinating music and the muscular control of the body. "It bound reason and emotion together and expressed them, through music, in physical movement." [6] From the beginning the drama was to ask questions about human existence and human destiny. The theater where this took place brought together masses of people and became a great social as well as educational institution.

The great festivals of Greece lasted for several days, with two or three days given to the dramatic contests. These began at daybreak and continued through the day. The winning playwright was crowned before the audience and was highly respected by the people. The open air performances in the great arenas demanded the use of masks and a chorus as well as song and dance to illustrate and emphasize the words of the play. The Greek chorus acted as an "ideal spectator." Arion of Methymna introduced spoken voices into the chanted dithyrambs, and some hundred years later Thespis decided to hold a conversation with his chorus and thus become the first actor.

In one century Athens gave the world four of its greatest dramatists. Aeschylus (525-456 B.C.) was the eldest and in many respects the most somber and magnificent. His plays are filled with foreboding and doom. Of the ninety plays attributed to him only seven survive. He introduced the second actor, differentiated the chorus and the actors by costumes, and elevated the actors by a boot which was called a *kothornos*.

A priest—as were Aeschylus and Euripides—and a man of great affairs, Sophocles (496-406 B.C.), wrote what critics have often called the greatest tragedy of all time, *Oedipus Rex*. The story and characters of the play have meaning for twentieth-century America. His *Antigone*, too, has been adapted by playwrights throughout the history of drama, and his plays have occupied the contemporary stage both in Europe and America.

Euripides (fifth century B.C.) won his first dramatic prize at a city Dionysia when he was thirty-nine. He is generally considered the most modern of the three writers and is often called a writer of psychological drama. Certainly he is the most contemporary in the way his plays delve into the motivation of men; his tragic heroes are no longer merely the victims of the gods or of their fates. He carried the drama a step further not only by celebrating the greatness of his fellow men but by exploring their shortcomings. He seems to have wanted to bring in a new day of social betterment, of honesty, and of rights for all men. His plays are a kind of social drama.

Comedy in Greece came from the Comus song or revel which was often connected with fertility. In contrast to tragedy, comedy presented all of the action on stage. It had much more relation to the audience so that it became popular as a form of commentary on manners and morals. It burlesqued many of the conventions of tragedy such as the use of the messenger, and it gave the audience a sense of participation in what may have been the thought of the spectator that had never been expressed. In this sense comedy is more closely related and intimately concerned. In Aristophanes' *Knights* Demosthenes says:

"Would you I told the story to the audience?" Whereupon Nicias replies:

> "Not a bad plan; but let us ask them first
> To show us plainly by their looks and cheers
> If they take pleasure in our words and acts."

Plato in the *Ion* classes the actor with the poet as an interpreter of the gods. "In like manner," he says, "the muse first of all inspires men herself; and from these inspired persons a chain of other persons is suspended who take the inspiration." The actors were looked upon as ministers of religion and their persons were sacred and inviolable.

In his book, *The Story of the Theatre*, Glenn Hughes gives this summary of the importance of the Greek theater:

> It can be readily seen that the theatre held an important place in Greek life. Its motives were religious, patriotic, educational, and aesthetic. Devoted in its early days to mythology, it came soon to embrace recorded history, and finally to interpret and evaluate contemporary life. Its tragedies plumbed the very depths of human emotion; its comedies subjected life to the most penetrating rays of human intelligence. Rising from orgiastic ritual during the sixth century B.C., it developed in the course of a hundred years into magnificent combination of poetry, acting, and pageantry. After the fifth century B.C. tragedy declined, but comedy persisted and flourished until the end of the fourth century B.C., when culture moved from Athens to Alexandria, and Greek civilization gave way to Roman. Probably the first well-organized theatre in the world, the Greek remains one of the most inspiring.[7]

The Roman world found its drama in wars and conquests, and the instinctive form of amusement was athletics. Classics of the Greek stage were performed in Rome, but they were altered to exhibit more spectacle and more entertainment. Seneca, one of the famous tragic dramatists of the first century, followed Greek models. Although he was popular during the Renaissance, it is doubtful if his plays were performed in Rome during his lifetime.

Rome liked festivals, and her games were called *ludi* or plays. She was also the originator of the circus where gladiatorial contests, animal fights, races, and gymnastics vied with each other for popular support. The remains of the ancient arenas where these took place can still be seen in Italy. By the fourth century after Christ the Roman calendar was mostly holidays—101 days were given to plays, 64 to chariot races, and 10 to gladiatorial contests. Rome loved the pantomime with the actors in masks and the mime which degenerated into a bawdy show that satirized almost everything.

Man's struggle with man, his absorption in the trivia of life, and his living unto himself in a society that gradually evolved into a mad, competitive scramble had its effect on drama and theater. The theater was soon to become the place where man's lowest and meanest characteristics could be seen. In his own natural weakness man liked to see the weakness of his fellow men. From the Greek theater—a place of worship in the time of Aeschylus—to the arena orgies of the later Roman theater is a long development. It is the history of a theater that ceased to have serious and significant meaning. It represents the dilemma of much of the theater today, but the story of this modern development deserves more elaborate telling.

When the theater had degenerated until its effect was only to divert man, a new force had arisen in the world. In the catacombs of Rome little bands of men and women formed an underground movement that advocated a new way of life that stood above any government which might try to impose limitations upon its adherents. In the struggle that was to grow around the early Christians the world was to see the material for new drama. The earthly life of Jesus, the moving spirit of this new interpretation of an old religion, was dramatic. He stood out against the powers of a corrupt secular world; he lived as if God were not some remote force or some idiosyncratic human-divine idol, but a father, the Being who had brought him into life, who provided a world for his food, shelter, and protection; truly the kind of father who would search all night if his child were lost. This Father God of Jesus was an indwelling spirit that lifted all men into a new relationship and that made each life sacred and of equal worth. Here was a concept of man and of God that was to create dramatic struggle as it came against the crude life of the later Roman empire. It is still the material for drama as it comes against the ruthlessness of modern society in the world as we know it.

By the time of Tertullian or by the second century the leaders of the new religion had come out against the institutions which were disregarding the worth of human personality and were corrupting men by exciting their sensual natures. The theater was one of these institutions. Marcus Aurelius sat publicly in his box but averted his eyes to a state paper or a book. Arius, the leader of one of the greatest heresies of the early church, talked of setting up a Christian theater in rivalry to the pagan theater. In his *De Spectaculis* Tertullian said:

If the literature of the stage delight you, we [Christians] have literature in abundance of our own. . . . Would you have also fightings and wrestlings? Well, of this there is no lacking, and they are not of slight account. Behold unchastity overcome by chastity, perfidy slain by faithfulness, cruelty stricken by compassion, impudence thrown into the shade of modesty: these are the contests we have among us, and in these we win our crowns. But would you have something of blood too? You have Christ's.

Tertullian called the theater the devil's church. The later church fathers and Augustine, specifically in his *City of God*, distinguished between high and low drama and praised the use of high drama in education. In A.D. 400 he said, "The theaters are falling almost everywhere, the theaters, those sinks of uncleanness and public places of debauchery."

The early Christians are often given credit for the destruction of the theater. The truth is that the world was changing and with it the theater had to change. The Lombards came in 568, and after that the theater really ceased to exist as an institution of any consequence. "The drama as a living form of art went completely under at the breakup of the Roman world. A process of natural decay was accelerated by the hostility of Christianity, which denied the theater, and by the indifference of barbarism, which never imagined it." [8]

Remarkably little connection seems to exist between the classic stage of Greece and Rome and the medieval drama. For most historians the medieval drama represents a new beginning. The wandering minstrel, acrobat, juggler, or wild-animal trainer took the place of the actor of the Roman theater. The street was the natural place for these amusements. At the same time, however, religious poems were composed. The Dark Ages are dark only by comparison with more brilliant periods of history. One of the surviving representatives of the early religious poem is *The Harrowing of Hell*, written in dramatic form but probably intended to be read. Dramatic dances, folk games, and folk plays also existed from a very early period. The May-day games and dances, as well as the more formal morris dances, come from very ancient times.

Plays connected with these—particularly the Robin Hood plays—were improvised as mummings. The mumming of Saint George in the Saint George play is a typical example. They are genuine folk plays. Roswitha, the Benedictine Abbess of Gandersheim in Saxony, emulating Terence, wrote six plays in Latin for the edification of her nuns. These were written to be read, not acted.

Medieval drama is usually said to originate in the Church. Part of the ritual of the early church is characteristically dramatic. The ritual of Gallican origin, used at the dedication of a church, is an interesting example of this early dramatic form.

The bishop and his procession approach the closed doors of the church from without, but one of the clergy, representing the evil spirit, is inside. Three blows with a staff are given on the door and the anthem is raised: "Lift up your heads, O ye gates; and be ye lifted up, ye everlasting doors; and the King of glory shall come in." From within comes the question: "Who is this King of glory?" The reply is given: "The Lord of hosts, he is the King of glory."

Then the doors are opened, and as the procession sweeps through, the evil spirit who was concealed within slips out. The dramatic expulsion of the spirit of evil takes place so that the church is consecrated to God and purified through the use of holy water and incense. The host is then introduced and the altar becomes a sacred place. In the Roman Catholic Church such was and still is the finely dramatic service that opens a church.

E. K. Chambers in The Mediaeval Stage says:

Dramatic tendencies of Christian worship declared themselves at an early period. At least from the fourth century, the central and most solemn rite of worship was the Mass, an essentially dramatic commemoration of one of the most critical moments in the life of the founder. . . . Some scholars attempt to show that the earlier gospel narratives of the passion, those of Saints Matthew and Mark, are based upon a dramatic version . . . on classical lines, and to have been performed liturgically until about the second century, when it was dropped in deference to the ascetic views of the stage then prevalent. The gospel narrative is, no doubt, mainly a "presentation of dramatic action and dialogue. . . ." The earliest liturgical dramas, even in the Greek Church, and those only guessed at, are of the fourth century.[9]

Antiphonal singing seems to have been introduced into Italy from

Antioch by Ambrose of Milan. It is from this antiphon that the actual evolution of liturgical drama starts. Often the melodies used in these antiphonal exercises were not sung to words at all but to vowel sounds. Then texts were written later. These were called tropes. The earliest extant tropes are from the ninth century and are found in a manuscript which shows that the monks of Saint Gall had improvised words to the old liturgical chants. Later in the same century, Benedictine monks added action to part-singing. The method was extended to the Christian story, to other parts of the New and Old Testaments, and to the lives of the saints. The *quem quaeritis* of Easter Day is the finest example.

We can imagine how this early trope was written. Probably one Easter season some of the younger brothers went to the Superior to suggest that on this great feast day some additional feature should be added to the regular service. The superior, being a stickler for tradition, told the young men that they might sing something additional— an extra number for the occasion. Despairing lest they might not get to do even this, they decided to accept the offer and worked out a choral addition to the music of the introit of the Mass, that is, the procession with which the Mass began. The addition was an instantaneous success.

The following description of the trope used at Winchester around A.D. 970 will give some idea of its simplicity:

While the third lesson is being chanted, let four brethren vest themselves. Let one of these, vested in an alb [a white linen vestment], enter as though to take part in the service, and let him approach the sepulchre [a place on the altar, bare except for the cross, surrounded by a veil] without attracting attention and sit there quietly with a palm in his hand. While the third response is chanted, let the remaining three follow, and let them all, vested in copes [hooded cloaks], bearing in their hands thuribles [vessels with incense], and stepping delicately as those who seek something, approach the sepulchre. These things are done in imitation of the angel sitting in the monument and the women with spices coming to anoint the body of Jesus. When, therefore, he who sits there beholds the three approach him like folk lost and seeking something, let him begin in a dulcet voice of medium to sing *quem quaeritis* [Whom seek ye?] And when he has sung it to the end, let the three reply in unison, *Ihesu Nazarenum*. So he, *Non est hic, surrexit sicut praedixerat. Ite, nuntiate quia surrexit a mortui* [He is not here. He is risen, as he said. Go announce that he is risen from the dead.] At the word of this bidding, let those three turn to the choir and say *Alleluia! resurrexit Dominus!* [Alleluia, Christ is risen!] This said, let the one, still sitting there, and as if recalling them, say the anthem *Venite et videte locum.* And saying this, let him rise, and lift the veil, and show them the place bare of the cross, but only the cloths laid there in which the cross was wrapped.[10]

This simple action proved so popular that the dialogue was enlarged and some real dramatic action was included. Finally the action was divided into scenes, and then other characters were included. In one version Pilate places a watch before the sepulcher, an angel sends lightning, and the soldiers fall as if dead. Then the Marys appear and sing songs of lamentation. One scene introduces a spice merchant from whom the women buy spices to anoint the body, a character who was to become humorous in a still later version of the play in Germany. At first the properties were extremely simple, for example, a pile of service books on the altar for the tomb. There were no costumes to distinguish the characters, although later both costumes and other realistic accessories were added.

One of the happiest examples of medieval drama is the play *Adam* which dates from the twelfth century. This play, divided into three parts, treats the fall of man, the first shedding of blood, and the fore-shadowing of the redemption. Its unity is religious but not dramatic.

The miracle play *Daniel*, which dates from 1140, has had some successful revivals in New York and Boston in recent years.

The popularity of the trope caused some trouble. At Christmas time the same technique was introduced, and at Holy Innocents' Day and Epiphany dramatic performances were added. Ascension plays became part of the repertoire. Finally, to give more room for the staging and to allow more people to see, the priests presented the dramatizations in the open yard where platforms had been erected. These spaces, too, became crowded; therefore, the plays were taken to the streets and market places. The church could not hold the crowds, nor could the Church keep the secular and humorous elements from being introduced. When the plays left the church, they began to include a great many scenes that had no place in the church. The separation of the Church and drama was taking place. For many hundreds of years thereafter, the drama, which had begun originally in religious rites and had been resurrected in the worship of the Church, stayed out of the Church.

When drama left the churchyard its control passed to the municipal authorities and into the hands of lay groups which were called guilds. These fraternities of men pursuing the same crafts took over the plays, each guild performing one of the scenes in the longer plays. The plasterers put on a play, *The Creation*; the shipwrights did *The Building of the Ark*; the fishmongers and mariners, naturally, were adept at *The Flood*; the goldsmiths were a natural for *The Adoration*; and the bakers worked at their own trade to put on *The Last Supper*. The language was changed from the Latin of the Church to the vernacular of the country. Scenes that had no relation to the Bible were introduced into biblical stories. Herod and Pilate became very important characters; Noah's wife became a shrew; and Mary Magdalene became the heroine of elaborate shows of profligate luxury. The plays of the Church were secularized, nationalized, and localized. Likewise, in the metamorphosis they became theatrically effective. They were genuine folk plays.

In order to show the various parts of the play in sequence the guilds put the scenes on stages or wheels. These pageants usually had two floors, the lower for the dressing room and the upper for the stage. On great feast days, such as Corpus Christi, the plays formed part of the procession. Finally, the lower part of the wagon became the place for hell. Great cycles of plays were shown in one day. The York plays are a cycle of forty-eight plays and were all given on one day, with the performances beginning at four-thirty in the morning.[11] Plays on saints' lives came to be called miracle plays.

No sooner had the liturgical drama been taken up by secular groups than the Church began to realize the danger in what had happened. Opposition was set up and grew in intensity. In an anonymous sermon in 1375 these arguments for and against miracle plays were given:

Arguments for: (1) Played to the worship of God. (2) They do not pervert but by force of example turn men to God. (3) Move men to tears and this in turn leads them to compassion and devotion. (4) They often lead those men to God whose hearts have been proof against all other approaches. (5) Men must have some sort of relaxation, and miracle plays are better than other kinds of amusement. (6) It is lawful to paint pictures of miracles; it is lawful to act them; the dramatic method is more effective for teaching holy Scriptures.

Arguments against: (1) Played not to the worship of God but to the approval of the world. (2) Men are converted by miracle plays just as evil can be cause of good, i.e., Adam's evil cause of Christ's coming. More people perverted than converted. Plays are condemned by Scriptures. (3) Men weep, not for their own sins, not for their inward faith, but for their outward sight. It is not, therefore, allowable to give miracle plays but reprehensible. (4) Conversion is an act of God—motive for conversion can come from miracle plays, but only feigned conversion. If truly converted would hate such playgoing. (5) Recreation should consist in doing works of mercy for one's neighbors, not in false vanity. Wicked deeds of actors and spectators prove plays' worthlessness. (6) Painting, provided it is true, Christian and restrained, may be as a book to discover truth. But acting is an appeal to senses. Good men, seeing that time is already short, will not want to spend it in playgoing.[12]

In the course of time moral allegories in the form of plays came into popularity. These were called morality plays. Personifications of virtues and vices were used as characters. The Seven Deadly Sins, Charity, Flesh, Learning, Mind, Will, Youth, Age, Holy Church, and Riches are all characters found in this type of play. The earliest morality recorded is a dramatization of the Lord's Prayer, Paternoster, dating from 1387. The play is concerned with the results of the seven deadly sins and the petitions of the prayer in the form of a contest for the soul of man between these sins and the Christian virtues. Everyman is the best example of the morality play extant. It has been performed continuously from the time it was translated from a Dutch play of the same name until the present time. The famous performance under the direction of Max Reinhardt in the cathedral square at Salzburg, Austria, the performance by E. Martin Browne in England, and innumerable productions in this country have made it one of the most often produced plays of all time. It is still one of the truly great plays that needs to find production in the Church today.

At a still later time, a new type of play called the interlude came into popularity. It is a play with two or more characters in which the author invents much more freely, uses comedy, sets his scene in the near and familiar, and is realistic. The farcical episode of Mak, the sheep stealer in The Second Shepherd's Play, is one of the happiest examples of this kind of play. The subject matter of this mystery play is the nativity story in which low comedy is used to interest the audience in the story of the birth of Jesus.

A medieval farce that should be revived is Maistre Pierre Pathelin by Guillaume Alécis. This comedy of situation is delightfully funny today when it is not overdone. It is a farce of subtlety and wit showing the knavery of Pathelin as a lawyer.

The transition from the humorous interlude to modern comedy is a natural one. Thus we see the play which began as part of the Mass pass through a popularization and secularization until it becomes a completely secular play. The farcical material which was used to enhance the religious part became the purpose of the play. With the plays of John Heywood, who was born before 1497 and died before the time of Shakespeare, the drama became the instrument of pleasure without serious or religious responsibility.

The history of religious drama from the beginning of the Elizabethan period to the present time is the story of the development of theater and the increasing richness of playwriting. Singular examples of great plays with profound meanings come to mind. Marlowe's *Dr. Faustus* and Goethe's *Faust* treat in different ways man's search for truth, the understanding of good and evil, and the need for redemption. Shakespeare's *Hamlet, Winter's Tale, Othello,* and *King Lear* are some of the world's great dramas that reveal new insights with each reading.

A study of Allardyce Nicoll's *World Drama* [13] with its numerous quotations from plays will show that many plays of genuine religious significance are found in England, France, Germany, Italy, Russia, Scandinavia, and Spain. The list of plays for reading and study in the Appendix of this book is a long one, but its richness only suggests again how many great playwrights have turned to the great tensions of life that have to do with man, his meaning, and his relation to values and purposes that are fundamentally religious.

The drama of the contemporary world beginning with Henrik Ibsen has often been called the drama of social significance because it has treated social problems as they are seen in the lives of ordinary men and women. Certainly *Brand, A Doll's House, Ghosts, An Enemy of the People, The Wild Duck, Hedda Gabler,* and *Rosmersholm* deserve the new translations and the fine revivals they are being given. They still remain the contemporary world's greatest plays.

Scarcely less significant is George Bernard Shaw (1856-1950) whose plays are now read for their cleverness and wit and for the profound comment most of them make on the strengths and weaknesses of contemporary man and his society. *Arms and the Man, The Devil's Disciple,*

Androcles and the Lion, Man and Superman, Major Barbara, and *Saint Joan* are all plays that provide delightful reading and enjoyable study.

John Galsworthy's problem plays are still valuable as sociological studies. St. John Ervine's *John Ferguson* has been called a kind of book of Job. Christopher Fry's *The Boy with a Cart, The First Born,* and *A Sleep of Prisoners* are beautiful, meaningful plays in a poetic language that is often dramatically alive. T. S. Eliot's *Murder in the Cathedral* and *The Cocktail Party* are two of the genuinely fine religious plays of this century. James Forsyth's *Emmanuel* and his version of Ibsen's *Brand* are becoming increasingly better known.

The contemporary Irish theater has produced poet-dramatists like William Butler Yeats and Sean O'Casey whose passion has been expressed in language that makes them two of the great artists of the present-day world.

France has continued to produce playwrights of astonishing versatility and power. Brieux, Rostand, and Becque have been followed by Jean Giraudoux, Jean-Paul Sartre, Jean Cocteau, and Jean Anouilh. The richness of the plays of these artists is hardly challengeable.

Gerhart Hauptmann's *The Weavers* was one of the finest examples of contemporary naturalism in Germany. Bertolt Brecht (1898-1956) came to international attention through his *Berliner Ensemble.* His concepts of epic theater must be understood to appreciate his plays. His is a theater calling for intellect rather than emotion, for directness rather than illusion, and for alienation rather than empathy. Critics agree that his *Mother Courage* may remain one of the great plays of the contemporary world.

Nor should one miss the plays of Karel Capek of Czechoslovakia, Luigi Pirandello of Italy, or Federico Garcia Lorca of Spain. Tolstoy's plays, together with those of Chekhov in Russia, complete a listing of European playwrights whose work should be read by anyone who wishes to understand religiously oriented drama.

America, too, has produced plays of consequence from the rousing propaganda of *Uncle Tom's Cabin* to the most recent plays of Thornton Wilder, Arthur Miller, and Tennessee Williams. Eugene O'Neill, Maxwell Anderson, Elmer Rice, Clifford Odets, Lillian Hellman, William Inge, Robert Anderson, William Gibson, Archibald MacLeish, and Edward Albee are familiar names to anyone who has read drama or attended the theater in America in the last fifty years.

With the founding of the Drama League of America under the leadership of Mrs. A. Starr Best, religious drama was revived in the Church, in schools, in colleges, and in the professional theater. The National Catholic Theatre Conference, the Religious Drama Project of the American Educational Theatre Conference, and the drama committees in two divisions of the National Council of Churches have continued and strengthened the movement. The pioneering work in the School of Theology and the Theatre Division of the School of Fine and Applied Arts of Boston University, the work at Christian Theology Seminary in Indianapolis, the drama courses offered at Union Theological Seminary in New York City, together with work at Redlands University and at Scarritt College for Christian Workers in Nashville, are evidence of the attention the Church is giving to drama.

What this new interest will mean is a matter for the future. Certainly, the concern of colleges and seminaries and the intelligent work of Methodist and Presbyterian churches is an addition to the interest in Britain where the Religious Drama Society, which has carried on for many years, has had the attention and respect of the professional theater, as well as that of the churches, for a long time. What this should mean is that the day of the concept of religious drama as the silly nightgown pageant in the church is over and that the new day of understanding the depth of religion and its concern for the good life is coming to focus in the drama.

Notes

[1] Glenn Hughes, The Story of the Theatre (New York: Samuel French, Inc., 1928), p. 8.

[2] For a fuller treatment of this subject see Melville I. Herskovitz, Man and His Works (New York: Alfred A. Knopf, Inc., 1950), Part V, Chapter 25.

[3] Quoted from George Cram Cook in the first program of The Provincetown Players.

[4] Hughes, op. cit., p. 4.

[5] For a provocative discussion of the origin of the theater see Benjamin Hunnigher, The Origin of the Theatre (New York: Hill and Wang, Inc., 1961). This is available in a paperback edition.

[6] Philip A. Coggin, The Uses of Drama (New York: George Braziller, Inc., 1956), p. 3. Used by permission.

[7] Hughes, op. cit., p. 78. Copyright, 1928, by Samuel French. Copyright, 1956 (In Renewal), by Glenn Hughes. All Rights Reserved. Reprinted by permission of the author and Samuel French, Inc.

[8] E. K. Chambers, The Medieval Stage (New York: Oxford University Press, 1903), II, 2. Used by permission.

[9] *Ibid.*, II, 3. For a more modern use of this idea see the *Passion According to St. Matthew* by J. S. Bach. The idea here dates from an early attempt to sing the Gospel and make it dramatic.

[10] *Ibid.*, II, 4.

[11] The whole of the forty-eight cycle plays condensed into an acting version was put on in 1951 at York in England under the direction of E. Martin Browne. The *Introduction* in Mr. Browne's selection of mystery and morality plays in *Religious Drama 2* (New York: Meridian Books, Inc., 1958) should be required reading.

[12] Coggin, *op. cit.*, p. 51. Used by permission.

This book is an excellent source for the history of religious drama and the attitudes toward drama by the church and churchmen.

[13] New York: Harcourt, Brace and Co., 1950.

Chapter VII

THE USES OF THE DRAMATIC

A. Drama as Celebration

IN THE ANCIENT WORLD MEN AND GODS AND THEIR DEEDS WERE HONORED by sacrifices and ceremonies in designated places. The Greek world was a world of such celebrations. To a degree this is true in the world where the Church has become the place for the celebration of events in the life of Jesus and the saints of Christian history. Great movements in church history for the Protestants, likewise, have been memorialized in services of commemoration.

An interesting example of this kind of celebration—among its other meanings and purposes—is found in the Protestant concept of Communion. The immediate friends of Jesus met to "remember" him in the Last Supper. Later the friends of the friends, the group of the fellowship of the followers of Jesus, met to commemorate his last meal with his disciples. As this ceremony was observed by taking food or wine and bread, the eating was done in memory of him. How interesting is the apostle Paul's statement of the meaning of the Communion: "As often as ye eat this bread, and drink this cup, ye do shew the Lord's death till he come." It was the core of early Christian worship, and it was a dramatic ceremony in every sense of the word because it was a *showing forth*, a *representation* of an event which had deep and real significance. It was an action performed. We *celebrate* Communion.

In the process of this development, confession of sins and forgiveness, as well as praise and thanksgiving, were made a part of the ceremony. Around this core of the service grew all the other characteristic aspects of worship. It was "right, proper, and a bounden duty" to give thanks. How pathetic it is that the contemporary Christian in the evangelical

98

church has lost his capacity to express thanks. He allows the minister
to do this for him. He is likewise limited in his ability to praise. He
sings songs of praise in a desultory fashion, and hallelujah sticks in his
throat. He finds no excitement in praising God and in expressing his
thanksgiving. Praise and thanksgiving are now largely offered by choirs
expertly trained musically to feel for him and express for him.

The Church must regain its function for celebration of worship if
it is to be unique as an institution. It must afford men a chance to worship, to give themselves in public corporate ceremonies to something
higher than themselves; it must allow them to express their feelings in
acts of worship so that the meaning of these acts will be constantly clear
and understandable to them. It is through worship that the dramatic
can re-enter the Church.

The Church must learn how to celebrate great historical events and
the personages of whom these events may be the long shadow. To celebrate an event is to dramatize its meaning. The European church has
been more effective in keeping these events alive. *La Festa el Missterio*,
held yearly at Elche in Spain on the day celebrating the Assumption of
the Virgin Mary, is an event in the life of the Spanish church. Anyone
who has been present to see the Virgin taken to heaven by being
drawn up through the dome of the church and has been part of the
shouting, laughing, and crying mob knows that for that time, at least,
something has happened, something has been vividly alive for several
thousand people. *The Mystery of Elche* is a dramatic reality, and it cannot be forgotten no matter what may be one's attitude about its theological implications.

The Church needs to regard baptism, marriage, admission to church
membership, and death as times of celebration. The meaning and purpose as well as the quality and means of celebration will differ, but
the fact of celebration will prevail. This is an instrument of the Church
which gives it uniqueness in a modern society.

Nowhere is celebration more likely to be needed than in the great
events of the church year. Christmas and Easter should be celebrated;
so should Advent, Epiphany, Ash Wednesday, Good Friday, All Saints
Day, Whitsunday, and the lesser days which have been dropped from
the "free church" Protestant calendar.

The reason why many of these days have dropped from the calendar
may be due to a lack of proper ways to celebrate them. The Church

has no real means to celebrate birthdays or what on the church calendar are called feasts. Here dramatic means can make a contribution, but it will need to be means that are not yet improvised. There is need to remember, and to remember by calling attention in effective ways to events in the life of Jesus as well as in the lives of the apostles and saints who have made Christianity the vivid, living thing it can be. Here again, Christianity has been demonstrated by these men and women, and the demonstration is something that the Church needs to see today.

Obviously, the lives of most of the saints are matters of legends and myths, and some of these are forgotten or at least have never been kept current for the Church today. Only recently has a writer in the *Saturday Review* suggested that the vitality of a religion can be judged by the freshness of its myths.

Lawrence Housman has kept the legends related to Francis of Assisi alive in the delightful *Little Plays*. The body of material relating to the events of the lives of the saints is enormous. Much of it is too ridiculous to be of any use, but again and again there are stories which cry out for dramatization.

Contemporary Protestantism is without the rootage of tradition, and particularly without the charming legends which make so vivid the meaning of much of the witness of its heroic figures. Furthermore, the evangelical branches of the Church have almost totally neglected the church calendar. As these events are brought into focus for one day, the Church has attempted to resurrect some of the meanings.

An example of this may be found in the revival of a day to celebrate the meaning of the Reformation. When the makers of curriculum began to probe into history and to find what events in the life of the Church, to say nothing of the life of Martin Luther, were available, they discovered that except for a feature-length film and innumerable books very little had been done with a subject that ought to be kept alive and fresh. Nor have denominations founded by exciting figures been any the more ready to celebrate the contributions made by these men. The Baptists have only recently looked into the highly dramatic life of Roger Williams, and the Methodists have looked, but have done very little about John Wesley or Francis Asbury.[1] Still more important is the need to give a sense of the Church to contemporary churchgoers. This can be done, in part, by celebrating the Christian year.

Christmas

Most Christmas celebrations in the Church are neither educationally sound nor dramatically effective. Merely to put into action the events surrounding the birth of Jesus is not to present an effective pageant or drama. A pageant may often lift a congregation because of its mass effects, its use of group movements, and its pictorial devices.

What we should celebrate at Christmas time is what Jesus of Nazareth stood for. We commemorate his birth by rededicating ourselves to what he taught. What could be our finest dramatic celebration has been made into a rather meaningless, sentimental celebration of the birth of a baby and the attendant wonderful events that surrounded it.

We can give thanks for the advent of Jesus by the use of drama and music which glorifies and interprets the significance of the life of Jesus. The traditional carols can be used to show the extent to which the birth of Jesus has affected the world.

There are a few good plays to be used at Christmas. They should initiate worship experiences which grow out of thinking and out of emotional reactions that remind us of the meaning of Jesus for us. Christmas must be made a day for considering the worth of individuals and also of the family of all the children of earth to whom a man came to bring a gospel of peace and good will. Simple scenes relating these ideas to contemporary life can be given. Projects which look to a better community, as well as to better world relationships, need to be emphasized. The season should be one of emphasis upon the value of each person and upon the need for concern on the part of all for every other creature. Pageants that show the effect of Christianity through the ages can be given. Music, drama, choral speech, and interpretive dancing are all ways in which the meaning of the religion of Jesus can be interpreted.

Lent and Easter

The Easter season is the most dramatic of the church year, but the events and their meaning for us are so great that we can scarcely condense them into one unified play. This is perhaps the reason why most of the Passion plays are undramatic. They try to give too much and usually succeed in treating much of the material with little thoroughness or dramatic intensity. Maundy Thursday has something to say that can come through no other day. Good Friday needs drama to give a sermon-interpretation of the tremendous events of that day. Easter Sunday should be the outburst of joy and thanksgiving that can come only when the spirit of God has so illuminated a man that he knows no death.

Drama can help to reinterpret the meaning of Easter and of Holy Week for the Church. Music, speaking choirs, and effective dramatization may call us again to follow the example of a completely consecrated man whose redemptive message for the Church needs to be heard now. The dramatic representation need not be given on the day of the celebration—it should be a part of the church educational process.

Drama in the Church must not be used to dress up an occasion merely to give it prominence or popularity. Drama should be a tool of the ministry of the people in the church who feel that their interests, capacities, and abilities can best be used through this particular medium. *It should be used any time when what needs to be said can best be said through drama.*

Many times during the year something needs to be said dramatically. Christian history is full of events that show the forces of light battling against the dark, reactionary effects of evil. From ancient times to the present men and women have lived lives that have stood against wrong. Sometimes their lives have been recognized, and they have been sainted. Other lives have been recorded in modest ways and with little publicity, but the deeds have stood. The contemporary church can lift up these witnesses to truth and justice through dramatic episodes in their lives and show the contemporary Christian what living in the Christian pattern has meant and still means.

Fearless prophets and more ordinary men today are trying to live their faith. The Church needs to give effective expression to the dramatic incidents in the life of Mahatma Gandhi, Toyohiko Kagawa, Albert Schweitzer, Jane Addams, Muriel Lester, and other men and women whose names are not so familiar but whose lives have given exciting witness of religious living. No better episodes for drama could be found than the intense moments in the lives of local figures who have been pioneers in just and honorable living.

B. Education Through Dramatic Production

Most educators agree that to be integrated, personality must be motivated by an ideal. For the Christian this is the ideal of a life that finds its source of power in God as he is revealed through Jesus. This means that each Christian can find a relationship to God and through the precepts and the example of Jesus can find a right relationship to man. The integrated personality is "at home" in the universe; it belongs. It should not, however, be satisfied with things as they are. Once a person has understood the meaning of the religion of Jesus he can never be content with what man has done to man. To become effective in changing the state of man, he needs to organize his own life into a harmonious whole. Education becomes for him the process whereby he gains a complete conception of life. As he sees life in this way and as he grows into an integrated person at the same time, he becomes an adult.

The growth process in personal and social education needs imagination to comprehend goals. The dramatic instinct is peculiarly the instinct that uses imagination, for it enables a person to put himself in someone else's place. The capacity to imagine the thoughts and acts of another person begins in earliest childhood in imitation. It is then transferred to the play stage—first with one's self and then with others—and finally it gives each older individual the ability to create characters while he is working in a co-operative group process. The more dramatic instinct is cultivated, the larger the perspective of the person is likely to be. He gains perspective by understanding other people. In this way he gains a conception of life that sees things in proportion, and he can more readily belong.

Religion needs imagination and the dramatic instinct. If we are to be persons who are sensitive to other men, if we are to relate ourselves to God, if we are to worship and pray effectively, we must have the capacity to imagine these things, for no matter how wide our contacts and our life span, we cannot know all of these things through direct experience. The ability to put ourselves in the place of others will alone help us create the brotherhood of man. How much insight with imagination it took to see a common fisherman and know that he could be Peter the disciple! How much understanding and imagination it takes at the present time to forgive one's enemies, and what dramatic instinct is necessary to sympathize with and understand the situation of people less fortunate than ourselves! To create a new world we must have these assets, for without vision a people will perish.

In the program of Christian education the need for the cultivation of the imagination and the dramatic instinct is at once apparent if we are to identify ourselves with life situations and have the vision to put them into action. All the fine sentiments which we accumulate in religious education will be wasted unless we cultivate the sense to see them in situations which most of the time do not exist except in imagination. Furthermore, to understand the past and to have a sense of its relation to the present is a matter of imagination as well as knowledge. The Bible is a book singularly lacking in exact description. Not even the figure of Jesus is described with accuracy. To reconstruct the person of Jesus through the records, imagination must be brought to bear upon the records.

In the presentation of the formal play the whole process can be an educational experience, and in the church it should also be a religious experience. This can only happen when we recognize that the uniqueness of drama in the church arises out of what the activity does, both to the actors and the production crew as well as to the congregation that comes to participate. Creating a character, no less than creating a scene or lighting a playing space on a stage, requires technical skill. Without a sense of the dramatic, however—the objectification of our dramatic instinct—imagination and creativity in the lighting and scenery still will not be used to best advantage. These, then, are the two primary prerequisites. If a child has grown up under the creative dramatic process, he will have both of them. He is likely to be the person who will also appreciate the insights of religion because he knows the way to actualize them in everyday experience.

One time we thought that educational dramatics was principally concerned with the people backstage. We said boldly that the play was being done for them and that if an audience was present it was inconsequential. Our purpose was to produce a play for the benefit of those who were participating as cast and as production workers. The director was concerned primarily with the development of these individuals, and the success of the experiment would be judged solely by their growth.

The project might be a simple play dealing with the concern persons should have for their neighbors—with the theme, let us say, of the Good Samaritan story. If the educational dramatic method worked, the person cast as the Good Samaritan would have been through a sound educational process; he would have learned not only the teaching of the parable, but also the historical background of the story. Every character in the cast would have learned something about the period of the play and would understand the ethical values inherent in the story.

This method is attractive and desirable largely because it means that persons with little or no ability may have an opportunity to act and to participate in the production. The idea is that the method can also allow a director less concern for perfection. Yet without the stimulation of an audience plays do not come alive nor can the "miracle of the theater" ever take place. Formal plays are not best suited to the educational technique. The creative dramatics method should be substituted for children and role-playing for adults.

A child or an adult creating any part in a play ought to go through an educational process. The depth and effectiveness of this process is determined by the depth of the actor's feeling as he assumes the character. It is also determined by the way in which the character is developed so that it becomes a reality both to the actor and to the participating audience. If the dramatic process for young people and adults does away with audience participation it lops off one of its most valuable potentialities. There is no consummation or completion in a performance until an audience comes alive to the play.

Since the production of a play is a group process, unity and focus can obviously be achieved only through competent direction. If each person in the production disregards the others chaos will result. Likewise, the selfish person will find that expression of his own desire must be submerged in the good of the majority. The young person who is over-assertive will soon understand that the success of the project will depend on his doing his part with a minimum of his habitual expression. Boys and girls who have never learned to work with other children will in time find joy in this co-operation. *The purpose of the play, not the director, should be the unifying element.* The enthusiasm and energy of the group can be captured in the ideal that has been set up. The director is the person who holds the group to this ideal and who helps each person achieve his maximum effectiveness.

Drama is being used in many types of therapeutic work. In a sense drama in the church is likewise used for this purpose, for in this kind of drama each person associated with the project is important both as a person and as a contributing factor in the co-operative process. In

ordinary play production when an individual interferes with the procedure because of personal shortcomings he is quickly dismissed. In our
use of the drama we must be determined to find a place for each person's
assets. We cannot be psychiatrists, nor should we attempt counseling on
difficult matters of personality adjustment. We do know, however,
that the process of producing a play can help even antisocial personalities
find a constructive outlet for their energies and a place in a co-operative
venture that makes all persons lose their individual selves in the working
toward final group achievement.

We know now that the educational process is as continuous a process
in the theater as it is in life. Nowhere is this demonstrated more effectively than in the growth of students in high school and college. The
drama gives an actor a chance to understand characters that can never
come into his actual experience. Through his imagination he may appreciate historical characters that by reading in a book he can understand
only dimly. He becomes the person while at the same time he has a
perspective on that person which actors alone can get. He must be able
to put himself into the life experience of a person whom he can never
possibly meet because of his restricted environment and limited experience. We have already suggested that drama frees an individual from
the confines of the narrow circle of his experience. Today he may
walk with kings, or he may feel the common touch of a person whose
social experience is completely out of his life. The good director is
the one who helps the actor and all of those concerned with the production to understand sympathetically and intelligently the background
of the play, the characters, and the experiences that they will interpret.

If the process of producing a play has been truly an educational one
the miracle of the theater takes place in that the audience joins with
the actors and the production crew in the experience of the performance
and in an amazingly short time goes through the experience of the play
firsthand. How good the educational process has been can be judged
by the sincerity of the actors and their capacity to "get over" to an
audience the thing that they represent—that is, to translate to the
people in the audience an experience in which they are participating.

If the director is forced to use persons who have little capacity to
interpret the parts, and if he knows that his performance is to be
ragged because he has tried to work with an inexperienced group, he
should then be bold enough to announce this fact to the audience. It

should not be done by way of apology, but it should be done as a matter of explanation so that there is no misunderstanding on the part of the audience as to what the director is trying to do. Every audience has the right to expect the best possible production of a play. Any performance that falls short of that standard must be explained.

Education during the process of production takes time. It cannot be done in a hurried, shortcut rehearsal period. It is in a real sense the method that is used in the continental theater, particularly in Russia. It means that all persons in the production are given chances. The director must be willing to work for long periods of time with the weaker members of the cast. He does not resort to typecasting even though it would be an easier method. Much more patience and understanding is required when the educational approach is used. In the professional theater typecasting too often is used largely because of the element of time, and because the director has neither the skill nor the patience to work with people who are less obviously suited to the character which they must create. In the amateur field the educational process simply means that in the entire project the person whose work is sincere, who is willing to work, and who is also willing to spend sufficient time will be rewarded by a director who in turn will try to help this person achieve the thing he sets out to do, so long as the production is not harmed by incompetence and lack of some ability. If the children used "show off," the process is not an educational one, and the resulting detrimental effects cannot be laid at the door of drama. The blame should be placed on the director for his lack of understanding.

The education of an audience is a new idea in the theater. In 1911 the Drama League of America was established specifically to educate audiences for better plays. The League had a playgoing committee which sent out criticisms of all the new plays. Local centers of the organization then took these comments to their constituency so that theatergoers could be aware of the type of play they were seeing. When an especially good play was given an audience was organized to support the play. This was audience education at a time when there were audiences for professional productions outside New York City.

In every church there are people who are willing to do something if somebody else will just take the initiative. The technical aspects of play production offer invaluable opportunities to get this kind of leadership.

Theater work has such scope that there is a place for each person, regardless of his interests or aptitudes. Then a group begins working together. The cutting out and sewing of costumes, the construction of a tree stump or a rock, the painting of scenery, the rigging up of lights, and the mimeographing of programs are activities which can be rich in co-operation, in recreation, and in the friendships which they foster. Under a skillful director many people can work together and have a good time all along the way if there is a common goal. The worth and the interest of the work can prove to be a forgetting ground for petty rivalry, self-assertiveness, and bickering which are sometimes present in churches.

The whole work of technical production can be made even more worthwhile if it is done regularly for other groups. The play can be presented before clubs, organizations, and other churches, or the stage crew of the church may pitch in and help other amateur organizations of the community in their productions. People find themselves in work to which they can give themselves. The scope of work involved in dramatic production is intriguing for many people.

If plays in the church are to succeed in being something more than shows the people who come to the play must be willing to help create the response that is part of the process. Only as they are aware of their purpose will the play come alive. The wise director will do everything possible to help in the education of an audience. If the play is an experiment, or if it is being done as a project in co-operative work, a short speech before the play begins can introduce the meaning of the project and can ask the co-operation of the audience. If printed programs are used some intelligent notes may point out the purpose of the play and its value as a project in the church. A drama group may also have "afternoons" when they can present informative talks on plays. The more understanding the audience has, the more certain will be the success of the play from a religious point of view.

We have said that the entire process of producing a play should be an educational project. If a play has values, if it is carefully interpreted, and if it is performed sincerely and intelligently before an audience that comes to enjoy the experience, it will inevitably be an educational process for the cast, for those who helped in the production, and for the audience that comes to participate in the experience as it comes alive.

C. Drama as Recreation

Our forefathers understood the meaning of "enjoy" as experiencing. Drama has the capacity to re-create through enjoyment. Its capacity to give perspective, to let us see ourselves as others see us is more evident when one assumes a role in a play. Through the portrayal of a character an actor is given insights into character that can come in no other way. The character must be brought to life. This means that the actor must live the character until he walks, talks, and feels like the person he is representing. This can be true recreation. To play is to become a part of, to re-create. Recreation through drama is a way of throwing one's self into life and not escaping from it. If plays are produced for recreation and by recreation is meant escape from life, the group will be disillusioned. Even a superficial characterization requires some understanding of life. Drama lets one see life and by seeing life understand contrasting values and concepts.

Drama for recreation allows one to laugh and to have the healthy, cleansing experience of enjoyment. Naturally, the value is conditioned by the kind of laughter. "Gypsy laughter from the bushes" is of dubious value. Likewise, laughter which arises from the exhibition of bad taste, of catering to sensual experience as a thing in itself, has no place.

As a group process "putting on a play" requires the time and talent of an amazing variety of people. That the production of a play can use all talents, that it is always a co-operative venture, and that it is successful only when everyone connected with it has had fun make it a contribution to any institution when these values are wanted. What must be stressed again and again is that the production of a play is not easy, that it will be disappointing and disintegrating as an experience unless time and ability are freely given. The better the play, the more expert the production, the more certain are the positive results. If a play is worth doing, it is worth doing well. The amount of recreation is proportionate to the amount of effort that is put into any production. There is no shortcut to worthwhile enjoyment.

Notes

[1] Information about the film on the life of John Wesley can be secured from United Methodist Communications, 1525 McGavock Street, Nashville, Tenn. Donald Mauck's play on Francis Asbury, *Glory in the Land*, can be secured from Dr. Mauck at the United Methodist Theological Seminary, Delaware, Ohio.

Chapter VIII

DRAMA AND WORSHIP—CHANCEL DRAMA

A. Dramatic Worship

DRAMATICALLY EFFECTIVE WORSHIP SUCCEEDS IN LIFTING THE WORSHIPER out of himself and in bringing him into the spirit or presence of something higher than himself. This may be from a source within himself or from something he feels outside himself. True worship establishes a relationship with this presence or spirit. The enduring quality of the relationship and the intensity of the reality are tests of the validity of the experience. In this sense, then, true worship is the recognition, identification, and relationship to the noblest, the highest, and the best that one can conceive. It is a coming into the presence of God and remaining there.

Worship is this relationship in progress. The effectiveness of worship can always be judged by the way in which the self is prepared for the experiences of this relationship to the highest and noblest and by the resultant effect on the self. It is, therefore, a two-way experience. It is the soul and spirit of the individual going out to a higher spirit, the opening up of the avenues of approach and, at the same time, the coming in of the influence of the greater spirit. Like all experiences, it is at first self-conscious. The more one comes into the practice of it, the more certain does the experiment become natural and spontaneous. It is always possible to have the experience of worship immediately and without even the consciousness of an attempt. When this happens it is one of the supreme experiences of life—a moment in eternity when the physical is broken through and the self enjoys a spiritual existence. As man succeeds in discovering this spirit world, as surely he must in his progress toward higher levels of living, the union and relationship with the supreme spirit will become the truly noble and energizing experience of his life. It will, of course, color every other experience and grow to be a more continuous process in his every activity of life.

The technique of practicing the presence of God demonstrated by Brother Lawrence is in a very real way perfection of the technique of practicing worship. Worship is an extraordinary thing or an unusual experience only because it is not continuous. In the progress of spiritual life it should become more continuous so that all life becomes a worshiping experience.

On the other hand, the very complexity of living, the distractions of the materialistic world, and the busyness of life are all characteristics that make the true experience of worship all the more unique. This does not mean that worship should be an escape or that it is a running away from day-by-day experiences. On the contrary, it should be the means whereby these ordinary experiences are given meaning and are elevated to the distinction all life should have. The necessity to "be still and know" is a prerequisite to strength, poise, and inward peace. As one prepares himself and comes into a relationship with the spirit of life he is participating in preparation for and the experience of worship. When the union between the spirit of man and the spirit of God becomes complete true worship takes place.

The dramatic is always the genuine because it arises from within and expresses itself in the truly sincere. It is always an experience from the inward outward. It is the expression of depth feeling. Its expression reveals its origin. Dramatic speech is characterized by its sincerity, by its depth of feeling, and by its meaningful expression. To test the dramatic quality of speech one must evaluate the sincerity of its origin as well as its effect. Like produces like. The dramatic should cause depth reactions. Deep calls to deep. The end of worship is so much a depth experience—in fact, it should be the deepest experience of life —that it should always be dramatic. *All effective worship is dramatic.* It arises out of a deep feeling of relationship, and it succeeds because it establishes that relationship.

The Leader of Worship

Unless the leader of worship himself is having the experience of worship there can be little hope for a worship experience on the part of an individual being lead. The leader must, therefore, feel genuinely everything he does. Through the experience he transmits his own feeling. He is not playing a role; he is not assuming a position. He is worshiping. He is part of a total process.

This means, therefore, that in group worship the worship leader must prepare himself for the worship period as surely as the worshiper in the group is prepared. Dramatic group worship can be effective only when the group itself is prepared for the experience and is helping in the participation. This same principle applies to all those participating in the worship—the assistants, the choir, the organist, and those in charge of seating or administering any part of the service. The entire personnel in leadership as well as those in the congregation must be in a unified worship atmosphere. Distractions caused by interruptions by insensitive worshipers can destroy the dramatic effectiveness of worship.

This is particularly true because dramatic worship is always unified worship which begins with the entrance into a receptive attitude and continues as the worshiper is raised to that point of unity and relationship with God which is the end of dramatic worship. It continues until the experience is completed. The object of worship should be the creation of an experience that can be carried out and continued after the group is disbanded. The more one becomes experienced in worship, the mcre fully he will learn the ways in which the experience is continued.

Dramatic unity is always achieved by recognizing a beginning, a rising action, a climax, and an end. These are not artificial markings. They are essential elements in the structure of a worship service. For this reason the place of worship, the establishment of the atmosphere and mood, the call to worship, the participation leading up to the climax of the moment of emotional and intellectual unity in the spirit, and the holding of that until it is established and becomes reality are all component parts of the total dramatic worship experience.

Ways to Dramatic Effectiveness

The setting of a worship service can be either dramatic or theatrical. If it is theatrical the trappings will call attention to themselves. A dramatic setting never calls attention to itself. It always becomes part of a total picture. When lighting, costuming, setting, and atmospheric conditions call attention to themselves they obtrude so that they distract from the purpose, and the dramatic element may be lost and the service may end in a theatrically impressive but superficial experience. Anything new may often be considered theatrical. It must be introduced with explanation and through an educational process. Changes in an accustomed service are oftentimes so distracting that they negate any chance for betterment. This does not mean that worship needs to be stereotyped or that changes cannot be made. The way in which they are made is important, however. Worshipers must be prepared for changes, or worship is likely to be theatrically exciting but not dramatically effective.

Dramatic unity which has the structure of a beginning, a rising action, and a climactic ending is not an artificial structure. The tone and intensity of worship should obviously not be the same at the beginning as at the climax. There should be rising action or intensifying feeling as the service progresses. The worshiper comes into the atmosphere and experience from myriad distracting influences. Each person coming into group worship is coming from a different kind of distraction. In the theater the lowering of the lights, the magic moment before the curtain rises when the audience is stilled, the use of music, and the device of a curtain are all means to galvanize a group into a whole and to prepare it for a unified dramatic experience. The church has no such opportunities. Yet it must use lights and setting and create moods even more effectively than does the theater.

As the theater recognizes the distractions from which the audience comes so must the church. It should not ask people to come immediately from a distracting world into the sudden experience of worship. For that reason, if the congregation can be brought into a service at the beginning, the auditorium should not of necessity be dimly lighted nor all of the setting of worship completely established. If a congregation is friendly and chatty it is much better to introduce worship gradually. This can be done by means of lights or by the use of music or by the preparation of the altar or worship setting which will be the visual objects on which the worshiper will concentrate. The ritualistic churches do this by lighting candles after the congregation has assembled. If there is a worship setting the worship leader as well as the congregation should be facing it. Nothing is more absurd than the average Protestant procedure of introducing a worship setting and then having the minister or worship leader sit with his back to that setting. It should be the focal point to hold the attention of the congregation so that there is no distraction. Dramatic worship appeals to all the senses, for it is a complete experience. It appeals, therefore, to the sight and to the hearing. In certain churches the atmosphere is equally important, and the purification by holy water and by incense is not accidental.

Dramatic Unity

Dramatic unity in a service is related directly to the movement of the service. Once the mood has been established and the service has begun there should be a continuous development. The intensity may be relaxed at moments in the service, but the unity should never be lost. The qualities that will hold attention, direct thought, and supply the feeling of spiritual relationship must be arranged in logical progression.

The preparation of a group for worship has been grossly neglected in non-Roman churches. The preparation of the setting of worship, the establishment of a mood, and the call to worship are fundamentally important if the dramatic values are to be initiated. From distractions and noise to quiet concentration is the aim of the beginning of the service, for the service begins whenever the congregation is directed toward a setting and attention is concentrated on the purpose of the participation. The call to worship should be truly a call to worship. This does not mean a few mouthed lines that have little or no meaning to the congregation; it does not mean a superficial call. The call is dramatic only when it is genuine, when it pulls people out of their distractions and reminds them of the purpose for their being present. Here as much as any place in the service creative ability needs to be introduced. A good call to worship that has become established in a church can help enormously to bring about an effective total group experience. The individual preparation takes place in meditation and prayer.

A dramatic service will rely on experiences that are familiar to a congregation as well as those that are new. A familiar call to worship and familiar hymns have genuine value and place, just as certain litanies, creeds, and prayers have significant contributions to make. The introduction of new material can have appropriate significance because of the meaning of the day, the time, or the purpose of the worship. Obviously this is best illustrated in the use of the materials for Christmas, for the celebration of various days in the church calendar, or for the particular needs of the congregation.

Dramatic Prayer

Dramatic unity is accomplished also by the maintaining of a mood and a spirit. The offering can be as dramatically effective as the reading of the Scriptures and the prayer, provided it is thought through in terms of the mood of worship and of its place in the service. How it is introduced and carried out is, of course, of great importance. The repetition of prayers and the use of litany familiar to a congregation are not dramatically effective simply because they are well known or are repeated often. Their effectiveness will depend on the way they are repeated. In a prayer every phrase should be fraught with meaning and considered seriously, not ruined by meaningless repetition. The repetition of the Lord's Prayer should be one of the high moments in a service of worship.

A prayer can be theatrical or it can be dramatic. If it is words spoken to gain effect or to flatter the capacity of the leader to coin nice phrases it is of little value. The dramatically effective congregational prayer is one that is spoken out of the needs of the people, and it is said with sincerity and felicity in phrasing that comes out of effective praying. The success of the pulpit prayer is measured by the praying congregation. When the congregation prays with the minister the prayer is successful, and it is dramatically effective. For this reason, the great prayers of the Church are obviously better than individual attempts by the minister.

Inherent in a dramatic experience is the sharing process. Unless the worship group becomes one with the participants in the leadership of the worship, and unless there is a total shared experience, there is likely to be little dramatic effectiveness. Each person out of the mood and each person who does not succeed in becoming one with the total experience is a distraction. The leader may be the chief distraction.

B. Music in Worship

Music is not an adjunct to worship; it is a means through which one worships. The so-called mood music at the beginning of the service, like music in other parts of the service, should not be the occasion for the mere display of skills. It is the beginning of worship. Like the worship leader, the organist must be a worshiping participant. He must feel the mood, enter into the experience, and have the privilege of helping to direct it. For this reason, therefore, the music in the various parts of the service, forming almost a continuous structure, may be the foundation unifying all the service. Growing out of it but never separate from it should come the spoken as well as the silent meditative parts of the service. There is no place for prima donnas either in the pulpit or in the choir. Special numbers are a tragic holdover from the concert hall and are likely to be distractions rather than contributions to a worship experience. A solo can be expertly and technically effective and at the same time a genuine part of the worship provided the artist is a part of the experience himself. The choir as well as the soloists must be worshiping participants. When a soloist stands out from the group and when he centers attention upon himself and distracts the worshiper from the setting to the individual, the dramatic unity of the service is likely to be jeopardized. The organist, the choir leader, and the choir as well as the worship leader—who may be the minister or his associates—all play a part in the total dramatic unity. One is as important as the other if there is to be an organic whole.

Group singing can be dramatic or theatrical, or it can be merely meaningless activity. If it is singing that arises from the true spirit of worship and gives utterance to thanksgiving, to petition, or to an affirmation of faith, it can be an integral part of the service and heighten the worship to give effectiveness to the whole experience. The use of traditional folk music with religious overtones may have values for fellowship. It has no place in dignified worship.

All of these aspects of dramatic worship must be made important to the congregation through the educational process, through classes in worship, through instruction in the church school, and through practice in the main worship service. The main service, however, is not the place for untested innovations and experiments. The young people's meeting, the church school, family nights, and worship interest groups are the places where experimentation should take place. When a technique has been perfected until it is related to and becomes a part of the unity of the service it can be brought into the main worship service of the church.

Dramatic Leadership

Obviously the success of any service will depend upon the persons who lead the service—the minister and his associates, the choir, the director, the soloists, the ushers, and any others who participate in the activities of the service. Unless there is a common understanding and purpose in this leadership group there is little hope for dramatic effectiveness. This unity can be brought about through conferences, through discussions, and through the give-and-take that must of necessity be brought into the picture if there is to be a real attempt made to worship.

The worship leader, more often than not the minister or his associates, is the pivotal person. If he does not have a sense of the dramatic, if he has no real depth experience and does not understand worship, there can be little hope that the whole service will in any way be dramatically effective. If he leads in prayer it must be because he is praying. If he reads Scripture effectively it must be because he understands the Scripture, because he has read it and reread it, and because it has meaning for him which he wishes to transmit to the congregation. *If the spirit does not come alive in him it will not come alive in the congregation.*

This all applies with equal importance to the sermon. It can be an exhibition, a theatrical stunt, a dull academic recitation, or it can be depth thinking arising out of depth living spoken in terms of present-day life and experience measured by the witness and the revelation of the spirit of God. If the sermon is this kind of exchange of experience and is a real exposition of insight gained through consecration and study it is certain to be a part of the dramatic unity of the total worship service. The way it is spoken will either be distracting, theatrically annoying, or will evidence sincerity in its dramatic effectiveness. The Protestant pulpit has too often been the place for bombast, for ineffective and poor public speaking. Until the preacher is trained in speaking there is little chance for dramatic worship.

Dramatic Timing

In a service of worship there must be time for the experience to begin to find its place in the life patterns of the participants. If the service ends rapidly, if it is disturbed by people going out of the auditorium, if there is not silence and prayer, it is likely to be ruined at its most important moment. The most effective dramatic worship allows the heightened moment at the end of the sermon or prayer to have time to sink into the consciousness of the participants. The benediction, the offering, and the choral amen are all distinct attributes to dramatic worship.

This matter of time and silence is, of course, an important part of the entire service. Time has always been important in the theater, and so-called timing of speaking and action is one of the first techniques that is learned by an actor. In the church timing must be a natural, spontaneous thing. It must grow out of feeling and become effective because it has genuine purpose. The speaking of lines effectively may mean that they are broken in the center by silence or by inflections that give them heightened values. If this is done superficially it is theatrical. If it is done with feeling it is dramatic. Timing, therefore, in a service of worship is a matter of feeling the sense of the meeting. If a moment of silence after the prayer is needed it must not be neglected. This is a matter of testing, judgment, and feeling.

Silence is a dangerous thing. For most people silence is distracting. Only after long training can it be used effectively. More and more it is coming into Protestant worship because of the experiences of the Friends. It should be brought back into worship but it must be used with judgment; it can be so effective that there is no other device comparable to it, or it can be so distracting that it dissipates the entire feeling and allows the mind and emotions to wander. There is no rule for silence. Its use and its values grow out of the feelings one must have and the sense that a leader can gather in knowing how much is necessary. Nothing is more dramatic when rightly used.

Dramatic worship will grow through experience. It may take upon itself techniques that come directly from the need of the moment, but it is likely to be effective only when there is consultation, co-operation, and a continuous educational process. Dramatic worship is possible in the smallest church and in the largest congregation. Its success will depend upon how much worship is understood, how sincere the leadership is, and how much time and preparation are put upon this integral part of the religious experience. It is the most unique contribution that the Church has to make to the needs of people, for it combines the total congregational group experience with the spiritual relationship without which life is indeed poor. Unless nonliturgical Protestantism takes its worship more seriously and develops the opportunity for genuine worship experiences the Church will become, more and more, merely a social institution and will lose its most important contribution to society.

C. Using the Chancel as a Playing Area

The theater is the theater and the church is the church. Each has its own distinct function in our society, and each must make its contribution in its own form, revealing its purpose in its best expression. The church must never seek to become theater, nor must the theater preach. Yet both have contributions to make to each other.

Good theater is dramatic. It has the capacity to stir the emotions on a deep level through the imagination which is more than fancy and superficial make-believe. The Church—particularly the Protestant churches—needs to express its Gospel dramatically if it is to make the hard core of its revelations a living reality in the lives of men today.

The chancel of the church is the place for this inspiration. Here, through worship, power can be released that will enable men to make the Gospel come alive in their lives. The fact that the sermon is often thought of as the only instrument through which this power can be stimulated is evidence of the failure of the Church to use the dramatic elements inherent in worship. The Church has been robbed of means that have constantly offered themselves to religious celebration.

If the Church is a place of worship and instruction, shows have no place in the sanctuary. The parish or community hall used by church· members may have a stage or a playing area where good plays can be produced. As a means of providing wholesome and worthwhile recreation this is entirely legitimate.

A place set apart for worship should have been built for that purpose. It furnishes few aspects of a stage even though the rites and ceremony of the church are performed on it. It is a place of reality, not of illusion. Communion is most intense drama, and it is a drama that is participated in by everyone. There are no actors in sacraments or in general orders of worship. What is done in costuming, properties, and scripting is not to give a semblance of reality. Each costume worn, whether it be a choir robe or a vestment, is put on with meaning so that it becomes not a costume but a symbol in an act of reality. In real worship the spirit of God is present—not the illusion of his spirit.

For this reason drama performed in the chancel should be drama which invites all worshipers to participate. The processional, the act of genuflection, and physical evidence of praise and thanksgiving are most real when they are dramatically sound, that is, when they are actions which grow out of completely sincere motivation.

A place of worship should not be reconstructed as a theater. The play which comes alive in a chancel should be played in the chancel as it is, unless the chancel is ineffective for worship and needs reconstruction to be effective for its true function. This limits what can be done in a sanctuary. The physical limitations of a sanctuary must always be given primary consideration in planning any kind of dramatic presentation.

In many instances, however, the chancel may be used as a stage for appropriate dramatic presentations, depending on the attitude of the denomination toward the meaning and use of the sanctuary. If the chancel of a church is regarded as a platform for a sermon a play can be produced on this platform. Theater-in-the-round has shown us that backdrops, curtains, and footlights are not necessary for good dramatic performance.

Such productions require skilled technicians and even more skilled directors. When theater aids are taken away the actor becomes much more prominent. The quality of the acting is primarily important in any sanctuary play since the surroundings are more intimate and revealing than in the theater.

The direction in this type of drama is all important. If the play is to come alive in a worship setting the director must have a sense of worship. He must have a feel for the place that will give his direction a tone and quality different from that of a secular production. He must be a better director because he is conditioned by the place, and yet he must direct expertly under these conditions.

Not all plays with church interiors as settings are appropriate to give in a church. For example, the setting of Christopher Fry's A Sleep of Prisoners is a bombed-out church, not a sanctuary designed for worship. The right setting for this play is a stage. Similarly, despite its name, T. S. Eliot's Murder in the Cathedral belongs in the theater. Plays ideally suited for the sanctuary have yet to be written. A new technique may evolve when the conditions and purposes of the production are thoroughly understood. Movement may be the chief characteristic of this new form, with rhythmic movement as a distinctive contribution. The voice and the speaking chorus must play a much larger part. Music will come back as an integral part of worship, not as an accompaniment.

It is possible that the new form may return to some of the earliest forms of the drama in Greece and that an integration of the arts of dance, music, and acting may produce something which will be called chancel drama. Much exploration and experimentation are needed before we can define this type of drama and determine its contribution to religious expression in the Church.

Few plays have been written for sanctuary presentation. Biblical stories that have values leading to deep searchings of soul, as well as meditations, may be dramatically presented. *The Sign of Jonah*, by Gruenter Rutenborn, may be given in the chancel. With good actors and good direction it creates a mental and emotional situation that is both highly dramatic and soundly religious. *Christ in the Concrete City*, by Philip Turner is another play that can be presented in the chancel, though it is less direct and forceful than *The Sign of Jonah*. The medieval morality play *Everyman* is excellent in the chancel as an acted Lenten sermon.

Royalties: Authors are human enough to like to be treated kindly and to respond kindly if they are. It is as well to remember that not only courtesy, but the law, gives copyright-holders certain rights and controls. They have the right to be paid for the loan of their property, and they have a right to protect it from mutilation or other ill usage. Most authors have a very natural concern for what happens to their work when it falls into the hands of strangers. Their plays are far more to them than merely "property" (or even merely a livelihood); they are the offspring of their labor, their experience, and their imagination. But authors like nothing more than to share these things with those who show that they appreciate them. And the fact always remains that both you and the author want the same things on the play's behalf: that it shall be performed as honestly and as effectively as possible; that it shall reach the minds and hearts of its audience. Mundane considerations are certainly not everything, but sound business arrangements with authors, like sound rehearsals, are part of the necessary foundation upon which sound performances are built.

> —R. H. Ward, "Agree With Thine Adversary,"
> *Christian Drama* (Autumn, 1953), p. 14.

Part three

Chapter IX

STANDARDS FOR CHOOSING A PLAY

A GOOD PLAY FOR THE CHURCH IS NOT EASY TO FIND. UNFORTUNATELY, the Church has not been willing to look with sufficient honesty on the major problems of life so that they can be acceptably produced in the church with any general agreement. Drama should deal directly and honestly with problems; consequently, it may be somewhat disturbing. So was the gospel of Jesus in his day! The time is rapidly coming when the Church will be able to speak frankly, freely, and truthfully about sex, marital relations, the home, delinquency, war, exploitation, labor, imperialism, and discrimination of all kinds. The better plays of Ibsen, Shaw, Hauptmann, O'Neill, Wedekind, Arthur Miller, and Tennessee Williams discuss these subjects. Most of these plays cannot, however, be put on in the church at the present time.

To discuss conflicts that arise from the evils connected with these life situations calls for honest, straightforward attitudes. The attempt to treat them in any kind of watered-down, parlor-talk fashion makes them unreal; it accentuates the very thing that the person opposed to this subject wishes to avoid. This is not a plea for realism as such, nor is it a wish for a washing of dirty linen in public. Certainly it is not a desire for dignifying back-of-the-barn talk by bringing it into the parlor.

The drama, we must emphasize, is always real in that it seems real; yet at the same time it is always the art of illusion. Art is never real in the sense that a replica represents the actual thing, nor is it real in any photographic sense. It is always the real thing filtered through the imagination of the artist. In order to win audience response the group producing the play brings this realism to life by means of the art of production which includes direction, action, scenery, lighting, and costuming.

The good play is not shocking in any moral sense unless the audience is prudish to the point of disliking honesty. It is never real for realism's sake or just for exhibiting something that can be better produced as a replica or as a picture. A good dramatist aims at a semblance of realism. This makes the audience believe in the authenticity and veracity of the situation and of the characters because they have the appearance of reality. What is important is that the person in the audience thinks the action on the stage is authentic, that it does not offend his sense of truthfulness, and that it appears real to him.

Too many plays for the church are weak and vacuous; they are pale and insipid treatments of situations and problems that cry out for strong, forthright presentations. Furthermore, they lack dramatic effectiveness—that quality of drama which presents a problem in a conflict moment, carries it to a tense moment of decision, and then holds the emotions of the audience at this climactic state. This is characteristic of all emotionally effective drama. If a play lacks dramatic effectiveness it ceases to fulfill its unique function.

Plays that are dramatically effective are not easy to find. Scenes in which forces are pitted against each other and the audience is sympathetic to the one or the other make situations for good drama. The best plays have closely knit action so that they seem to have a tautness that is felt whenever any scene is diagnosed. Technically expert plays are so condensed that scenes often seem underwritten. Many so-called religious plays are overwritten in dialogue and complication of plot so that they lack the compression that will make them effective on the stage.

Many biblical plays seem unimportant and appear to have little relation to problems of the present day. We are not aroused, shaken, or inspired by them. They leave us cold. The cast and stage crews cannot get excited over them, and this means that the audience is never moved.

Some plays written to be performed in the church not only lack these dramatic qualities, but they are also preachy and moralistic. Nothing can —and should—kill a play more rapidly. The moral or the point of the play should grow out of natural or real situations, conflicts that are met constantly in life. Plays should never attempt to preach a sermon. They are different art forms and have a different function. They must demonstrate life situations through action.

A play must be chosen first of all with the needs of the congregation in mind. The play-choosing committee must try to understand what these needs are and how plays can minister to them. A play ought never to be chosen just because a director likes it. A director should like the play he produces, but he should like it because it meets needs and demonstrates situations which can be shown effectively in no other way, and he should make the group understand his enthusiasm.

What are the needs of the congregation? Let us suppose that the church is in a relatively prosperous neighborhood and that the members are in the business world or in professions. It is likely that this congregation will have little understanding of the problems of labor and labor unions. A need here would be for plays that show the situation of labor and its fight for collective bargaining and organization. In a city church there may be a need to know something about rural situations and farm problems. Also plays dealing with peace and with race relations are needed everywhere. These needs arise because of the little experience most of us have with groups or types of life different from our own. The director must use judgment in selecting plays on these subjects. They must never be merely propaganda plays. On the other hand, *Back of the Yards* by Kenneth Sawyer Goodman can arouse a smug community to think and do something about the conditions in the slums. Galsworthy's *Strife* and Shaw's *Major Barbara* used for reading may awaken a congregation to situations in the struggle of labor and capital.

The process of choosing a play can be a continuous process in a group. If the director of a group will guide the reading of plays so that the group is constantly looking for plays to produce the process can be a genuinely educational experience. Members of a drama group need to get into the habit of reading plays. The search for plays for Christmas should have started in January, and as plays are discovered they should be passed around for reading. Probably by fall there may be ten plays which for one reason or another seem suitable for the particular church and the particular occasion. By careful analysis at meetings of the group, a play can be selected for production. The group will have learned about plays and will understand the reasons for choosing the play that has been selected.

A further advantage of this process is that the director will learn much about the taste and judgment of the group and will know how great the need for educational development is throughout the production of the play. If the group should fail to agree on the selection of a play, then the director must exercise tact and judgment in making the final choice.

The director must have the privilege of saying what play should be done. The aid of the director of religious education and the minister may be needed, but their authority should be resorted to only in a case of a deadlock in choosing. They should know the play that is to be done and their support should be sought in the project.

Chapters in this book on "The Play" and "What Is Religious Drama?" should be read carefully. They give the chief characteristics of a play and indicate what is generally meant by religious drama. The following tests are to be used by a play-reading committee in choosing a play for production by a church group.

1. A good play is one which moves an audience to participate emotionally and to respond to the conflict.

2. The subject matter of the play should be worthy of the time and consideration of the actors and of the audience.

3. The plot and setting of the play should be so related or pertinent to an audience that the situations and conflicts will be valid.

4. The plot will begin at a point that will elicit immediate interest; it will carry the story to the place where the audience will feel satisfied that the particular episode has been completed. It is compact and knit together so that it holds interest.

5. The characters must have a reality which makes them believable to the audience.

6. The action must be honestly motivated. It should begin in the "midst of things," rise to a climax, and complete itself as far as the story is concerned.

7. The dialogue must seem right for each character. It must never seem artificial or oratorical. It differs from conversation in its economy of words and in its directness. It is never rambling or leisurely.

8. It must have literary merit.

9. A good play may present its ideas through humorous situations. The humor should always grow out of situations that are accepted as probable and natural. Improbable situations treated as probable create farce, while exaggeration leads to burlesque. The value of a play will depend on how well it succeeds in being the kind of play it is supposed to be.

10. It must come within the range of abilities, equipment, and purposes of the producing group.

When the group and the play-choosing committee has reviewed the tests for a good play and has familiarized itself with the dramatic technique so that standards of judgment have been established, the actual process of choosing the play may begin.

Anyone interested in drama in the church will always be on the lookout for plays and scenes from plays that can be used. Radio, movies, and reading will furnish ideas. An alertness to need is the one essential.

Catalogues of play-publishing companies should be in the library of every church group. New plays are constantly being published so groups will want to keep informed about the new announcements and releases. Significant plays in the commercial theater and new plays from publishers may be reviewed regularly at the meetings of the drama group. A special committee should consider this its main function. Plays should be discussed and filed with complete notes on reactions so that they may be referred to and brought up when there is a need for a play.

Playwriting is a profession which deserves adequate compensation. A playwright is dependent on income from the royalty on his play. The publisher of the play likewise needs to get some return so that he can continue to print plays. The net profit to a publisher on a playbook which sells for fifty cents is obviously small. If cast copies are bought the profit is a little larger. Since it is illegal to duplicate copyrighted material, copies for the entire cast should be bought.

The author's royalty is likely to be a sum that is small compensation for all the work he has put into the writing. Church groups are notoriously careless about paying royalty. Good plays should be paid for, and good writers should be encouraged to write plays that will bring adequate incomes. The royalty notice is usually found on the back of the title page of a play. If there is no royalty notice it is likely that the play has no royalty, but the director should write to the publisher if there is any question. It is deliberately dishonest to change a title of a play or to change the lines in any way so that the play is called a new version. It is dishonest to think of producing a royalty play without paying the fee regardless of the cause for which the play is produced. A religious or charitable benefit is no reason for waiving the royalty unless the author and publisher consent. The fact that tickets are not sold does not make any difference. Unless the royalty notice specifically says that the fee is different if there is a collection rather than a ticket sale the fee must be paid. Many plays are royalty free or have reduced royalty fees if there is no admission charge. This will be noted in the write-up of the play in the publisher's catalogue or in a play list.

Not to pay a royalty when it is stipulated is cheating a writer out of his honest wage. It must not be the practice of church groups. To change the attitude of publishers toward church groups on this matter is the duty of every drama-producing organization in the Church.

Chapter X

THE PLAY COMES ALIVE

WHEN THE PHRASE, "THE PLAY COMES ALIVE" IS USED IT IS NOT MEANT TO suggest that the script is dead. The script is waiting to be born, and it comes alive only when the director, the actors, the production people, and the audience come together for that magic moment which is known as the "performance." After all the work which has gone into a production it may seem strange to call the moment of performance magic. Yet, even though what happens has been planned and worked on by a co-operative effort on the part of a large number of people, the actual thing that takes place in the performance of a play is something of a miracle. This is not meant to be facetious, because the word is used by directors whose group is not ready to perform and whose feeling about the whole affair has been that if it comes off at all it will be a miracle.

Quite a different sort of miracle does happen when a good script comes alive before an audience in a performance. John Mason Brown says of Robert Edmund Jones that the "theatre for him [Jones] was always an exceptional occasion." Roy Mitchell described this as "miracle" and his meaning is the substance of his book, *Creative Theatre*. No matter how many plays a director may have done, each production is a miracle because no one quite knows what the moment of coming alive may mean. It is true that the director has seen dress rehearsals with the production functioning—the lights, the scenery, the costumes and the actors ready for the opening, but when the first performance takes place there is an audience, and with an audience present all aspects of the production take on new dimensions. What happens happens for the first time and will never be repeated again in exactly the same way.

129

What does happen? A play that has been a script, with dialogue and stage directions, becomes a living experience to be shared by the persons who have worked to make the words become flesh and live in the confines of the human experience that make up the plot of the play. A play, furthermore, that has been a script—a one-dimensional, flat surface with words in it—has become a three-dimensional reality. It has taken on proportions: A room is no longer a word, it is an illusion of a room, defined as playing-space, and it has dimensions and proportions. Yet it is more than a room; it is the room in which certain people have lived and which now lives—and only for this space of time—because people who were descriptions, and who were dialogue now move about and live through a tense moment in their lives. Rooms are strange things. One can see them in houses and admire them for their decorative values or historic witness. In a play a room may still be a room, but it will be the room in which Nora in A Doll's House has lived and from which she has broken away. Trees may fit every requirement for a forest; yet in the magic and miracle of the theater trees become more real, something more than forest because it is the forest in The Blue Bird or the trees of The Cherry Orchard.

Still more of the miracle is seen when an audience lends its imagination to what actors and technicians have created and another kind of creative experience takes places. Every lover of theater knows the magic of the moment when house lights dim and there is the hushed expectancy of an experience waiting. It is then that the sense of wonder becomes a reality and "an extension of life, not a duplication, a heightening rather than a reproduction" takes place. The world of any number of people is suddenly extended and expanded, and a new experience shared by new people takes place. No other art galvanizes a group of people and takes them together into such an experience. The only other experience similar to this is found in a service of worship, but because of the difficulty of joining together people with differing concepts and differing theologies the service may not unify, and the miracle of relating all of the persons to God may not take place.

What does happen in this miracle of the theater? The secret may be discovered if a consideration is given to the place and contribution of the director, what the actor furnishes, the work of the production staff, and other means that are used to bring the play to life.

A. The Director and Directing

A good director is a trinity—a technician-artist, a diplomat, and an organizer—and like a trinity, he is three in one, for he must be first of all, an integrator. It is in his imagination that the play is seen as a whole; it is he who sees it in its totality and in all of its parts. He works with a designer and technical aids to conceive the vision he has of the play. He must be able to share his ideas and to communicate with his technical staff. In the working out of the action, as well as in the interpretation of the lines, the director must know what he wants because he has imagined the action. With the actors he becomes a benevolent dictator, while he is at the same time a diplomat who knows how to listen to his advisors, to take what is good from their advice, and still to keep in his mind the overall pattern he is seeking to bring alive.

He is the pivotal person in any production. A good play imagined in action by a director is the epitome of theater. While it is hazardous and probably unwise to suggest it, the quality of dramatic imagination of the director is the most important prerequisite for a good production. It is the one thing necessary. Positions on stage, timing, and interpretation of lines can be worked out. If, however, the director is lacking a sense of dramatic movement, a sense of the dramatic values in a play, and ability to picture the total performance and know what is wanted from the play no amount of technical excellence or acting ability will be able to cover up the primary lack in direction. Too many directors are merely manipulators of actors in felicitous positions on the stage. Too many are merely absorbed in the interpretation of lines. These are important aspects of direction, to be sure, but they are secondary to the total dramatic unity. Unless the director has the capacity to envision this, unless he knows what he wants, then all the other techniques he may have learned will be frustrating to him. The director is an artist, and like all artists he must know his craft. This comes by knowing the fundamentals of play-directing and from experience in using them.

For this reason the contribution of the director in religious drama is all the more important. He is not producing a play to preach to an audience, yet he is working to express the deepest and finest meaning in the play. He is producing this particular play because he believes in what it has to say, and he wishes this to be said effectively as drama. He knows that the meaning must become an actual experience both for the actors and for the audience. In religious drama, therefore, he is concerned about meaning. He must decide on this by careful study of the play. The more subtle the play and the more it is good drama, the more certain must the director be of the meaning he wishes to actualize. He studies the play. This does not mean that he reads it superficially a few times. It means that he digests it, that he lives with it, that he pictorializes it in his imagination. It means that he lives with the story and the characters until they are realities to him. Unless they are real, imaginatively real, unless he is able to experience their situations himself, he will never be able to help actors bring them to life.

He begins by reading the script carefully. He tries to condense the point or meaning of the play into one topic sentence. He says, "This play is about such and such," and he then spots the sentence which seems to say this. He finds the scene which is the essence of this idea and decides that this scene is the heart of the play. He finds how the rest of the action contributes to the making of this scene. He traces the action of the play from its opening scene noting the way in which the dramatist relates the action to the climax. He studies carefully the relations of the characters to the action, what each contributes by the person he is and, therefore, by the words he speaks.

The director places himself in the milieu of the play, trying to understand the period and its meaning in the historical setting. He reads all he can about the period, especially books that make the period live. He investigates the manner and customs of the time of the play, resorting to books and, still better, to museums where he can see costumes and properties as they were. He knows that these are probably not to be reproduced but that they are to be simulated, to be represented in such ways that they will seem authentic.

He learns everything he can about the dramatist's interest in this play—why he wanted to write it and what he hoped it would mean to an audience. How fortunate he is if the play happens to be one of George Bernard Shaw's! In the elongated prefaces—many longer than the play itself—Shaw states his reasons for wanting to write the play and much of the mental process through which he went in the collecting of materials as well as in the actual working out of the plot. Even with these prefaces, however, there is still much research to do.

Histories, especially those with prints and pictures, encyclopedias, other plays of the period of the type, pictures found in histories of art, biographies, diaries, letters, essays, in fact, any form of recorded experience which will spur the imagination, are needed by the director.

The play may be written in a form that is peculiar to a period, or it may be experimental and, therefore, without precedent, or it may seem novel only because the director does not know other dramatic forms from which it derives its novelty. How significant, for instance, are the styles of some contemporary continental plays when one knows the technique of the Nō plays of Japan, or how illuminating can be the understanding of the free techniques of contemporary dramatists when one knows the well-made play of the nineteenth century and can see the straitjacket from which it is a revolt.

A sense of the history of drama is necessary for any director who wishes to actualize the greatest meaning from plays. To produce a contemporary comedy one should know the types of comedy that have been historically important. To direct a contemporary problem play one should know the difference between the effect of tragedy and the effect of the presentation of a problem in which character has been sacrificed to the need for statement of the problem. One needs to know what epic drama means—and especially Shakespeare—before one is able to comprehend what Bertolt Brecht has done. Certainly one needs to know the tradition of melodrama if he is to understand the escapist drama that occupies much of the contemporary theater comedy and the television soap opera.

The director needs to be an observer of life, keenly aware of the nuances of character, yet not so absorbed in the idiosyncracies that the common and universal qualities are overlooked. He needs to know people both from the inside, where he finds motivations for actions, and from the outside, where he observes and records in his memory the action patterns that make people unique. He is an alive person, above all a sensitive person, so that he feels and knows through experience when an action is authentic and when it is bogus.

The director must be able to communicate his sense of these things by the most subtle methods known, perhaps, only to the theater. Directing is easy when a director merely shows an actor what to do. How many amateur performances are evidence of a director who has told the actor how to say a line and has directed his action so that it fits into a pattern, whether or not it is intelligently felt and thought out! The good director communicates by creating emotional and intellectual problems, and when the actor is not getting the right approach stimulates him by creating questions that he must answer if he is to find satisfaction in the part. This is probably the most difficult aspect of direction, for the director may discover that the actor does not have the capacity to comprehend what is wanted, or he may lack the sensitivity to feel what must be felt. The director cannot create these qualities when they do not exist, but he can so stimulate that the actor will go far beyond what is expected of him or what he thought he might give. When this happens the process is truly educational.

A director must be constantly growing if each play is to be actualized for its greatest values. If a director decides after a successful production that he knows how to direct he may stop growing. Each play is a new direction problem, and each play challenges the director to new insights and new imaginative experience. The director can learn basic concepts of stage positions, but the mastery of dramatic movement is a matter of visual imagination and feeling for pictures that is gained by trial-and-error methods, if, to begin with, he is given a sense of the dramatic.

The repetitive use of the phrase "sense of the dramatic" has not been unintentional. Its meaning ought to become clearer as one understands and feels the meaning of theater and the dramatic form in its expression. It has to do with mind as well as imagination; it comes about through experience as well as through insights and inspiration at the time of production; it grows from understanding plays through continuous reading of plays and through the habit one must form of visualizing the plays when they are read. A director always sees each play as a stage performance, and his mind becomes the stage. This truly is the "theater in your head." Yet theater is never realized until it is out of your head. This process the director guides, and this process is the "borning" of a play; the technicians and all the other related people—including the audience—are the company of wet nurses, as well as the "relatives," who participate in the birth with imaginative expectancy.

The director in the final analysis must be a person who can work through people. He works with the people in a cast, to be sure, but his most important job is to work through them. What he works through them is the play—the story and the characters—so that these are filtered through the actors and the production people to become what has been referred to as the miracle of the theater. The capacity to work through people means, as has been pointed out, that the director does not give direction to be carried out nor action to be imitated. His work involves both of these under certain circumstances, but basically he creates through people, motivating and expressing through them what he sees with them in the script for the audience to experience imaginatively.

All directors must have concern for the personalities of the actors. In the church this ought to be one of the major aspects of the director's job. The production of a play in the church should always be an educational experience because the people participating are usually amateurs in the obvious meaning of the word. They are often people with no experience of theater, not even as audience. They are amateurs not because they love theater but because they have a feeling that they might like it. Their knowledge of acting is in terms of movie stars or television actors who seem compelling and attractive. They are probably the people who say, "But I don't have any ability. I'd be scared to death to appear before an audience." Yet here they are offering themselves as actors in a church play. The director needs a keen insight into the personality of the actors as well as into the characters who are to come alive. *Both must come alive if the play is successful.* Often the director will find that his main and too often his insurmountable problem is that he just does not have people with enough sensitivity and imagination to be actors. He must work with what he has, good and bad. He can feel for and relate himself to the actors, but he cannot make them into artists.

What does he do? If the actors are so inexperienced that they cannot even learn basic techniques of acting in the time allotted for the rehearsal of a play he can suggest that the play be done as a reading and that the major emphasis be put on interpretation of lines. He can suggest that a simpler play be done first, perhaps only for the members of a group or for friends of the cast, and that this be a learning experience for the actors. He can steel himself to go on with the production, with the understanding that a note will be put in the program or a prologue with a humorous meaning will be added to the performance to say that this is a first attempt and that, whatever its faults, it is the result of serious and sincere effort. Dramatists of the past have been fond of explaining through prologue situations that they think ought to be faced, and they have asked the audience to be kind.

The text of a play may have to be edited or adapted to the peculiar situation in the church. This does not mean that it may be warped into the meaning desired nor that the realistic language may be watered down to fit the moral climate, whatever that may be, of the church. There is in some contemporary plays language which is strong and possibly offensive. Some changes may be necessary. Here taste and judgment are the only criteria. The fewer changes made, the better. It is true that plays may often be simplified in production by combining scenes or by cutting. In general, this again is a dangerous procedure. It is much better to do the play by simplifying the scenery so that a forestage can be used and the scenery kept to a minimum. The use of screens and platforms is advisable. More will be said about this under production.

Good books on directing are available to be studied. The important thing to remember, however, is that directing, like swimming, can be learned only through experience. The novice should begin with simple scenes, progressing to longer plays only when basic concepts have been thoroughly tried. The director has perspective on the play; he sees it as each person in the audience sees it. No actor, regardless of the quality of his imagination, can comprehend the total scene; or even if he develops a complete sense of his own role he cannot also visualize the other actors in relation to him. While experienced actors sometimes assume the position of director of a play, this is dangerous and risky for even a more-than-competent actor.

The primary direction of any play is dictated by the plot and the suggestions of the dramatist. In Shakespearean plays practically the only stage directions given are exits and entrances. The rest is left to the imagination of the actor and the director. With the open-ended stage of the Elizabethans, only the presence on the stage of the dandies and the rabble in the pit—our orchestra seating section—confined the actor.

Stage directions in any play are conditioned by the playing space which will eventually be used. How important it is, therefore, to define this space and the physical characteristics of the scene from the beginning of the rehearsals! This should be understood at once so that the actors know precisely the area in which they will work.

Most significant both for the director and the actor is the delineation of character basic to the plot of the play. This must be given primary consideration for it is the essence of the working arrangement of the whole play. The director needs to become so familiar with the script that he has lived it in his imagination. He sees it with his inward eye, as well as in the visual picture. He is constantly aware of the picture that is created while the actions are creating the situations in the play.

The director must also understand the play in terms of its rising and falling action, where emphasis is to be placed, and where pointing up needs to be done by his direction. The director can be compared with the leader of an orchestra. The musician knows the score, but it is the director who guides him so that he does not play too loudly or go too slowly or too fast. The director hears the play as well as sees it, and it is his ear as well as his eye that guides the harmonious movement of the actors.

The play director guides through the comprehension and understanding of the actor. Through consultation at the beginning of the rehearsals and throughout the play he leads the actor into a relationship to the character that requires concentration and genuine devotion. He helps the actor realize the role not by manipulating him but by directing him to an understanding of it.

Blocking is a word heard constantly in the direction of a play. It indicates the positions and movements of the actors within the playing space so that audience sight lines are good, and the actors' movements do not block each other from the sight of the audience. Blocking should be done only after the play has been read and discussed and the actors have a picture of the movement and understand what it means in relation to the story or plot of the play. Blocking is necessary because inexperienced actors cannot see themselves; they cannot feel deeply the parts they are playing if they must think constantly about where they are and how they are turning. Once the actor knows his relative positions on the stage he is free to think about and become the character he is portraying.

The director is always dependent on several other persons related to the production. A stage or production manager is responsible for all the physical properties on the stage. He sees that the scenery is ready and is placed so that it can be changed with expedition; he is familiar with the movable properties, and he organizes a crew to get props on and off a set; he checks the costumes to see if they are what the director wants; he works with the light technicians to see that the light plot is carried out and that the cues are on time. He is a very important person on whom rests the efficient running of the play. He may make the promptbook unless it is done by the director.

Sometimes a director is given an assistant who acts as a liaison person with the stage manager and other crew chiefs. He may be given the responsibility of the prompt book and may call all rehearsals and in some cases take over line rehearsals and individual coaching when action and interpretation have been established by the director.

In the church the backstage duties are usually assumed by committees which in the theater are called crews. In the professional theater these separate crews are in charge of stage and shop work, the building of sets, and stationary props; the electrical crew in charge of lighting; the prop crew in charge of all movable props; the costume crew; and the front-of-the-house crew. In churches there should always be a public-relations committee which has to do with the publicity for the performance. The business aspects of the project can be handled by a treasurer or a business manager. No matter how small the production, a comprehensive budget should be drawn up, and all persons related to the play should adhere to this budget in consultation with the director and the business manager or treasurer.

B. Casting

Casting a play in the church may be one of the most difficult aspects of the project. Too often the director in a church is told that Mary or John should be cast in the play because he has been faithful in attendance or has been tireless in his attention to duties in other projects. What the director knows is that he must use whatever acting and technical ability is available. Most of the time there is little choice except in the major roles. Here there may be a problem. If the play is to be performed before an audience and is sufficiently good to warrant the effort it takes, then the best possible cast should be chosen. This does not mean that actors should be recruited from the outside or that the same leaders must of necessity be cast again and again in a play. It may be the very thing to develop workers who have not discovered an interest in other kinds of work. In the last analysis, however, the play deserves the best acting and the best production possible, and persons must be chosen who can fulfill their oblgations.

While it is true that all work in the church should have educational as well as religious values, it is apparent that a singer must have a trained voice before he is asked to sing in a church service and an actor or technician must have ability and skills that can be developed. If the

Christmas pageant requires only pantomime and a minimum of that while music and reading are used, characters may be chosen who "deserve" parts, and the director can cast the play with only size and carriage as factors. In any case, with young people the director of religious education and/or the minister should be consulted before casting is announced. It is possible that the best actor may be the most serious problem child. It may also develop that casting him in the play is the way to find his loyalty and direct it. Good judgment with a good amount of trust and faith are prerequisite to any skills of the director, and the capacity to size up situations and handle them is as necessary as any knowledge of directing techniques.

The value of the play and its best performance must be given first consideration if it is to be done before an audience. In the process of production the skillful director can contribute much to the lives of the persons involved in the production, and by minor parts and by all sorts of duties connected with the staging, growth in responsibility and in talent can be encouraged so that the project can have genuine educational as well as religious significance.

The play may be the "thing" in the sense that it must come alive, but unless the people in the group process come alive for richer, fuller experience under the capable leadership of the director, the project in the church is not achieving the best results. The director in the church is first of all directing people—both the persons in the play who are waiting to be born and the persons who as individuals will bring the characters to life. In this sense the whole experience is one related to people, and the person who directs must first of all be a person of unusual quality. In the educational process perhaps no one is so closely related to the people with whom he works as is the director of a play.

Not the least important asset needed by a drama director is a sense of humor. The church group works on a voluntary basis. It may be made up of old and young. It is often working on borrowed time when actors and crews are tired. It may be made up of young people who have not been initiated into the serious business of producing a play. They are probably in the project just for fun. The director is the person who must have sufficient perspective to understand all of these things, to appreciate them, and yet have the patience to "let down" with the group and then pull them back up again. He must be able to laugh with the cast when the release of laughter may save the situation. He should

know that a good sense of humor may be the most effective means of in-
suring discipline that will keep a group at work. The steady grind of rehearsals or crew work can be lightened by it. Whatever else may be
prerequisite to directing, a sense of humor is a saving grace.

The director must feel himself a part of the institution through which
he works. The belonging sense is fundamental if the drama program is to
be related to the general educational program of the church. Furthermore, the director needs to know the congregation. The intelligent minister would not preach without knowing something about his congregation. Yet directors in the church are often asked to produce a play
without any knowledge of the congregation. The result is that the
play usually fails to come alive at the crucial moment of performance.

The church should not build its program on the work of those experts who make one contribution and then lose interest. The church
must learn how to compel the concern of experts—of artists of all kinds
—so that they make their contributions willingly. No apology need be
made in asking for their services. The giving of one's talent, ability, and
experience to the church should be a privilege. It should be a distinctive
part of the stewardship which everyone ought to feel.

Knowing an audience personally and having a sense of audience relationship are quite different. The director, to direct, must have this
sense of audience relationship. Until the audience is actually present,
their needs and tastes rest with the director alone. Seasoned actors will
have a sense of the audience, but most amateurs lack it entirely. How is
the audience sense acquired? Certainly one of the best ways is experience gained by being in an audience. Therefore, the good director is
one who has spent many hours sitting in audiences; he has watched not
only the show but also the reactions of the audience. For him the lines
of Emily Dickinson are delightfully true:

> The show is not the show
> But them that go.
> Menagerie to me
> My neighbor be.
> Fair play—
> Both went to see.[1]

If drama in the church is to succeed in stirring a congregation this
audience sense is imperative for the director. In the church the congre-

gation-stage relationship has greater significance than in the regular amateur or professional theater. If the director in the church is to succeed in "putting over" his play he must know exactly how he wishes the congregation to be affected.

The good director producing a play in the church will be cognizant of both the means and the ends which he uses—one must not suffer at the expense of the other. The educational procedure of rehearsal and the religious impact of performance are both to be preserved. While adequate attention given to the means will demand more time and patience, the effort necessary for the effective, determinative quality of the end will be worthwhile.

The church is part of community life. This means that all its activities must be considered and evaluated in terms of their contribution to community values. The director must have this community sense if the project is not to be dwarfed into a little outlet for a clique in a church. If the Church is to have a sense of mission—without which it cannot truly exist—this popular activity of drama must be considered as integral to this mission. Drama should bring people with all types of skills into the church in the producing group, and into the audience it should attract persons who might never come to the church for any other reason. This then makes drama an outreaching arm of the Church. The director should be aware of this if he is to make the most of it. One danger of drama in the church is that it becomes an ingrowing process that is thought of as the interest of a small and often smug group. A good director should be community-minded and should have a sense of mission to give the experience of a play to the largest group possible.

Of course, no one person will have all the qualities of the director analyzed here, but this fact will not discourage the dedicated director— it will spur him. As he grows, he can foster more growth for those who come under his direction. As he fosters their growth, he expands and intensifies the whole ministry of the Church.

C. The Promptbook

The promptbook of a production is an essential aid. While it is true that most churches are not likely to produce the same play within a short period of time, it is also true that the keeping of a promptbook will help everyone related to the production. If for any reason the director or the stage manager cannot be present the promptbook becomes an invaluable asset. Because it contains any cutting or changes made in the text, it is used as the source book if minor characters are without books.

The promptbook should be made up of nine-by-twelve pages with one page from the printed copy of the play pasted on each sheet. Two copies of the printed play will be needed to make the promptbook. There should be wide margins on all sides of the text, with the inside and bottom space used to note movements, positions, changes in text, tempo, and interpretations. In the top and outside margins should be written warnings for entrances and cues for lights, curtain, music, and sound. The prompt cues should be in different color pencil than the directing changes and cues.

The book should include carbon copies of rehearsal schedules, the scene and light plots, the property lists, program notes, publicity releases, and photographs. If a church takes its drama program seriously, these books will be added to the library and will be available for lending to other churches that may want to do the play.

D. The Actor and Acting

The actor is the center of attention in any play. His creative work differs according to the style of the play. His chief assets are sensitivity and intelligence, or what the great nineteenth-century American actor Joseph Jefferson called "the warm heart and the cool mind." An actor is an artist whose basic material is himself—his body, muscles, hands, feet, and voice. The Russian director Stanislavski divided the work of the actor into two spheres—the work on himself and the work on the role he is creating.

Pantomime was perhaps the first dramatic action in the world. Men acted out an idea before they put it into words. Acting was probably the first art of communication learned by man. Certainly, in the theater acting antedates the written play. As we all know, many profound emotions can be easily represented in action, but to give them words is indeed difficult. The obvious and yet most interesting example is the emotion of love, which can be naturally expressed by action, and yet can be very awkward and oftentimes foolish when it is expressed in words. Christian in Rostand's *Cyrano de Bergerac* was breathless in the terrible emotion he felt for Roxanne, but he was not poet enough to express himself. The charming love scenes in *As You Like It* are further examples of the same dilemma.

The kind of acting that grows out of premeditated planning is the kind needed in drama in the church. It must always be action which results from thoroughly worked out ideas motivated by deep and real emotion. Superficial action has no place in the church, nor has representation. Acting in a play in the church, therefore, becomes something more than a technique. It must truly be an experience. Its sign is sincerity on the part of the actor.

How then are we to get actors who are willing to take the time to study and understand a character in order to bring about this kind of action? Understanding must come first if a character in a play is to come alive. There are no insignificant characters in drama in the church. The smallest part is a reality or nothing. It must be thought through so that it becomes part of the larger pattern of the play. If it is badly or superficially done it will weaken the whole play. Characters in a conflict situation at a climax are so closely woven together and so interdependent that the failure of anyone weakens the whole structure. If this is not true the technique of the play itself is bad; it will not hold together, much less hold the interest of the audience.

Acting must always be more than acting; it must be interpretation. If a character is to come alive, he must be something more than the skeleton structure of words and positions on the stage. He needs the studied action that gives him life—the intellect and the emotions both adding to his quality. Interpretation, likewise, is something more than saying words well. Interpretation means bringing out the subtleties and the nuances that give idiosyncratic reality to a person. Parts in plays must become persons. The dramatist can give only the words, and while these may be entirely adequate to give an idea of the character, in the last analysis the actor makes the character become a person.

The material of a part is filtered through the mind and imagination of the actor and of the director. The play should be read carefully at least four or five times just to get the total picture. One of the great faults of the amateur is neglect of preliminary study for the relation of his part to the whole.

The amateur imagines that a casual reading of the play will supply the meaning, and that a line-perfect performance will be a successful one. He will soon learn that the better the play, the more care must be taken. The part to be created must not be considered as a part to learn; it is a part to be brought to life. This is no easy matter, and it cannot happen unless the actor is willing to spend a great deal of time understanding the character and the part the character lives. Everything about a character must be known. How he looks, walks, talks, sits, stands, gestures, eats, relaxes—all these must be known completely before the creative part of acting can begin.

What a man says is important, yet one only needs to think of a person he himself knows well to realize that what his friend says is merely an outward and audible indication of the real person. The actor must imagine the character outside the play as well as in the play; he must know background. Certainly he must know what the character would do in many different circumstances. The wise director will spend a long time talking out the character with the actor. Too often the playwright gives too little of the character. This always makes the actor's job much more difficult. Tragically enough, learning lines is often the only accomplishment of the actor, and plays in the church too frequently have unreal characters who speak lines but never actually live the experience. An audience must feel impelled to respond to the actor. It cannot do this in the religious sense if the characters in the play are not created by the actors.

The process of creating a character is not a simple one. An actor must live with his "part," and he must live with it intimately. This requires time, and it means that long before a part is learned it must be understood. The actor needs to walk and talk the part. He must give himself to it with a devotion that is rare in amateur drama. If our problem were simply to amuse an audience superficial acting might be condoned. If our theater were an escape from life, as some theater and movies are, the job of acting would not be difficult; however, when we propose to affect an audience so that it is elated and inspired, then the work before us is of great importance. Sincerity, honesty, and understanding will call forth that sort of response.

The actor's art, however, is not all good intentions, nor is it merely sincerity and understanding. He must learn to watch people, to see their reactions. He must be awake to living people if he is to create them on the stage. He must be willing to take time to think about the character until it becomes quite familiar to him. This process begins and continues by reading the play again and again. The character is from the play, and it must never be unrelated to the circumstances that gave it birth. An actor will always need to know more about the part than is given in the play. He will need to understand the environment, the setting, the way of life of the times, and all the historical relationships possible.

Most of us can act characters who are like what we think we are like. The problem of understanding characters who lived at times about which we know little or nothing is still more of a problem. For this reason plays founded upon biblical material are very difficult to interpret. To create a part like the apostle Paul the director and the actor will need to do research, to read books about Paul and his times. The more interesting and exalted the character, the greater will be the problem of the actor. In Oberammergau the citizens of the community are selected to take the roles in the Passion play by popular ballot. If a woman wishes to play the part of Mary she needs to live so that her neighbors will elect her to the role. This is a process of understanding that reaches into the living of people and calls for interpretations that are not artificially taken on in the hurried days of preparation for the play.

The actor needs to remember, too, that he is playing only a part of a whole; acting is always a co-operative process that can never be at its best when a prima donna usurps the stage or plays alone to an audience. The days of this sort of conceit are passed and should never be revived. Each person in the entire production is important to the finished product. By playing together—because the play is a closely knit unit— the achievement of an artistic whole is possible. This capacity to play with others is one of the truly educational aspects of drama in the church. The egocentric actor who is concerned only with his own success has no place here. Plays in the church need people who are willing to sacrifice all their selfish ends for the greater good to be accomplished by the play.

The Russian theater furnishes an admirable example not only of ensemble playing but also of the group process at work. The Moscow Art Theatre will spend months and even years bringing a play to life before it is ready for an audience. In this theater all people are important. The theater is an educational institution as well as one designed for entertainment. The peasant can get the idea through a play if the play is so well done that it will have precisely the desired effect upon the audience.

When the Moscow group was rehearsing Gogol's *Dead Souls*, for example, one scene was given an extraordinary amount of attention. Some twenty actors were on stage seated at a banquet table stuffing themselves with food and drink. The story of the play deals with the tax abuse and the old system of tax collectors. Into this banquet scene, unannounced and with alarming suddenness, walks a collector. Each one of the guests must register by his action and facial expression what his conscience feels at the appearance of this man. Guilt, innocence, unconcern, scorn, fear, threat—each of these must be shown according to the reaction of the individual, and it must be shown immediately. A long, careful analysis was made of each character seated at the table. Many of the actors had no lines to speak, and a large number did not appear in any other scene. Here was a problem in acting. To see the Moscovites work on the scene with the patience of truly great artists, to see them go over and over the action until each character was as nearly right as possible, is an experience which makes a person realize what is required of an actor.

Almost anyone can act if he acquires the techniques and comes under good direction. He may act, but he may not act well. Almost anyone can play tennis, but the Davis Cup winner is a player who has practiced longer than most people know, has had the discipline to make himself work, and has worked with coaches who know how the game should be played. The great player will still have his individual serve and his way of receiving the serve; he will always be the product of all his playing and coaching plus the something which is distinctively his own. So, too, the good actor will learn by doing, by understanding the technique, and by studying all that can be learned about acting. The average amateur will not be a good actor under these standards. Yet the more he can be encouraged to try, the more the quality of playing in a church will be raised. Good books on acting are available and should be studied carefully. Practice scenes are valuable for the beginner.

Although much good advice on technique can be learned from books, the actor must have the guidance of a good director. Most amateurs have not learned how to stand or how to walk—in other words, they are awkward. Acting shows up all these defects, so the director will watch the person's posture and his ability to use his body gracefully and expeditiously. The actor must be able to make his body do what he wants it to do. Awkwardness is unnecessary for anyone, and even minor physical defects need not keep one from acting. Some of the greatest actors have noticeably bad defects. To overcome these, the interpretation needs to be all the more subtle. Simple physical exercises will help. When a group can secure leadership, eurythmics is invaluable to help gain control of the body and to rid it of stiffness and awkwardness. High-school and college groups are giving much more attention to posture, and in many instances eurythmics is part of the physical-training program.

A good voice is equally necessary for the actor. Americans are likely to have ugly voices largely because they have never taken the trouble to train them. The voice, like the body, can be made effective by practice. Almost any community can find a high-school teacher who has had work in voice training. The person should be prevailed upon to work with the group. Choral speaking and speaking choirs are excellent ways to create interest in voice work. The actor should realize that his training must take in the total person—the body, the mind, the voice, and the personality. To create characters, all of these must be trained.

No substitute can be found for training and for hard work. Acting is not something that one does just naturally. Some persons have more than average ability to mimic. Nevertheless, even this talent needs training if it is to be an instrument in the co-operative process of bringing a play to life. The most supple body, excellent voice, and fertile imagination will be of little use if the possessor of these assets is not willing to work extraordinarily hard. To gain any kind of efficiency in acting takes time. The amateur is eager to accomplish what for professionals has taken years of work. In Russia the actor, like the ballet novice, begins as early in life as possible. The training continues all his lifetime. Madame Chekhov, the wife of the great dramatist and one of Russia's Honored Artists of the Republic, at seventy was still willing to take minor parts to get new insights into characters. To have this opportunity, she said, enabled her to get perspective on the leading characters. This is the attitude of a truly great artist.

The actor needs to learn how he can best memorize lines. Before the actor turns to work on actual lines his major work on characterization should be completed. If he were to speak in character impromptu, he would know the right pitch, tempo, cadence, rhythm, dialect, or speech provincialism of his character. Most actors find the job of memorization easier and more dependable if they work from general familiarity to specific line memorization. If the play is in three acts, the competent actor will first familiarize himself with all the play. Then he will pay particular attention to his lines. He will then become familiar with his lines by acts and by scenes.

At the same time he memorizes the idea or thought behind the dialogue. The grasp of the thought will pull the whole act or scene together for him. It will facilitate the actual memorization of words. It will enable the actor to enter into the real purpose of the scene. It will prevent him from forgetting "which line comes next." His thought throughout the entire playing of the scene can be given to the point of the scene, not to fumbling in his memory for the exact word. Only after these steps in the memorizing process have been taken is the actor ready to become letter-perfect in his lines. Most actors find they memorize better by "walking it out." This technique has an integrating quality; it pulls together the movement and action of the play, the bodily manifestations of characterization, and the actual speeches. It prevents one's remembering that he should walk to the table, pick up the book, and say, "So this is the new book." Instead, in his subconscious mind he has routed his movement to the table, and as he moves toward the table in performance, he can't think of anything but the line which motivated the movement. This walking helps make for thinking which motivates movement and the consequent speech explaining the movement. Most actors also "talk the lines out loud to themselves" as they memorize. This utilizes the sense of sound in memorization. After all these steps have been taken actors learn their cues so that the sound of these words calls out their speech.

The drama group should devote meetings to acting, to trying out scenes that have been selected for that purpose. Katherine Kester's *Problem Projects in Acting* is a valuable book for this purpose. It gives short scenes from plays that can be used for the various problems in acting. The organization that makes up the drama project should spend many of its meetings in this kind of activity. New recruits can be used in this way, and abilities may be discovered. The group should have in mind constantly that it is a workshop organization and that its time between plays should be taken up with training for the various aspects of play production. A drama group should be working continuously yet with interest and devotion which will be characteristic of the people who love drama and believe in its distinctive contribution to the Church.

To sum up, then, the group should start its training in acting by simple exercises in patomime—the expression of fear, anger, pleasure, distrust, love, and other emotions. These lead naturally to scenes from plays. Part readings of plays for the sense of the character are always advisable, and walking rehearsals will help in the understanding of what make a play dramatic and how characters can come alive even in this crude process. When the actor begins to feel at home with a character, or as if the character "belongs," then the art of acting is becoming real. An actor will soon learn that all action in a play must be motivated. There is no other kind of intelligent action in a play. Actors simply do not move at will. Every action has a reason or it is not valid. Part of the skill of the actor is to discover the pattern for action and, with the director's aid, work that into the total picture of the stage. That the actor works with the whole group cannot be said too often. The director is concerned with the action so that its flow in the performance is smooth. In the church the actor is the interpreter who knows that through his creation a character will come alive to affect a congregation of people and carry them with him through common experiences.

Notes

[1] From *The Poems of Emily Dickinson*, edited by Martha Dickinson Bianchi and Alfred Leete Hampson, published by Little, Brown and Company.

Chapter XI

ORGANIZATION AND REHEARSAL SCHEDULE FOR THE PRODUCTION OF A ONE-ACT PLAY

THE SITUATION: THE DIRECTOR OF CHRISTIAN EDUCATION OF A PARTICU-lar church has interested the Commission on Education in the use of drama in the annual Christmas celebration. They have enlisted the assistance of Mr. Stanley, a young businessman who has had experience in a college dramatic group. The following is the procedure which Mr. Stanley, the director, followed in producing the play for the Christmas celebration.

Procedure: First Mr. Stanley confers jointly with the minister and the director of Christian education to establish exactly why the play is wanted and what is expected from the production. This meeting is held on Saturday, November 3, and several dates are suggested by the minister as possibilities for the production. In order to give the maximum amount of time the tentative date of Sunday, December 23, is set for the performance. From this meeting comes this statement of purpose:

To add a fresh enthusiasm to the yearly program of activities of the Christmas season.

To involve the entire church membership in the performance.

To use this first endeavor as a sort of inquiry into the possibility of establishing a program of dramatics in the church.

The next move is to announce the plans for the project to the entire church membership. A space is given in the church newsletter which is mailed in time to reach members before the weekend of Sunday, November 11. The announcement is given on that Sunday morning and to various groups meeting in the evening. This is the announcement as it appeared in the weekly newsletter:

THIS YEAR'S CHRISTMAS CELEBRATION TO INCLUDE DRAMA

In addition to our annual Christmas music by the choirs, this year we are reaching out into a new area of the fine arts—drama. Believing that this is the right time to provide such an opportunity for people in this parish who are interested, the Commission on Education has encouraged the production of a Christmas play for this season. We are fortunate to have the assistance of Mr. Stanley, who has accepted the responsibility of the direction of the play.

If you are interested in being a part of this production in any way, will you attend the first meeting of the project on Monday evening, November 12, at 7:30 P.M., in the church auditorium? If you are interested, but are unable to attend this meeting, notify Mr. Stanley between the hours of 5:00 and 7:00 in the evening at his home, CE 8-9078.

Remember, there are many jobs connected with the production of a play beside those of the actors—costumers, painters, electricians, publicity people, and especially the audience. In other words—there's a role for everyone in our parish.

Choosing the play: On the evening of the first meeting, Monday, November 12, the director takes charge. He passes out mimeographed forms which he has prepared in order to get information concerning particular interest and ability of those attending the meeting. The form contains this basic questionnaire:

Name: Vocation:
Address: Phone:

Interests in drama: Experience in these:
   Acting   —
   Directing—
   Scenery   —
   Lighting   —
   Properties—
   Costumes—
   Makeup   —
   Publicity   —
   Other   —

Would you like to see a regular drama group formed in this church?
Further comments:

The director has chosen five plays which he thinks are possibilities.

The plays have been read and approved by the minister and the director of Christian education. The next step is the forming of a reading committee from this group, with each member of the committee taking one play, reading it carefully, and reporting on it to the entire group at the next meeting on Friday, November 16. The report should contain a description of the play as to length, setting, characters, and period; a summary of the plot; an analysis of the content and timeliness of the play and an evaluation of things most important in it; and a statement of its simplicity, difficulty, and suitability for this church.

On the evening of the second meeting, November 16, nearly all the people in the original group are present to be part of the work of choosing the play. The reports on the plays are given and after discussion—and not without subtle advice from the minister and the director of Christian education—the play is decided upon. The director then conducts a reading of the play, making certain everyone who wishes to read a part is allowed to, and announces that the cast will be decided upon from this reading and will be revealed in a supplement to the bulletin on Sunday, November 18. The first rehearsal for the cast will be on the next day, Monday, November 19. At this second meeting of the entire group the director also determines the heads of the production crews and gives them the names of the people who indicated an interest in that particular aspect of the project. The director will shortly be meeting with each of the crews to outline the plan of work.

The director casts the play, and it is announced in the Sunday bulletin as planned.

Rehearsal schedule: The director knows the importance of setting goals for the production—every meeting, every rehearsal should have a purpose, a goal. But it is just as necessary to adapt to the accomplishments of each, so that the project steadily builds on what work has been completed. Care should be taken not to postpone any facet of production or rehearsal for long because all parts of the play must get attention.

FIRST WEEK

First Rehearsal—Monday, November 19:

Goals: Talk to cast about the policies of the director.
                  Set the rehearsal schedule.
                  Read the play.

Accomplished: All but two of the cast are present. This is a good time for the director to talk about responsibility to the thing to which these people have agreed to do. He explains that he knew about and had okayed the two absences, since they were due to previous engagements that could not be broken. At this time he tells his people what he expects of them in the matter of co-operation and attendance at rehearsals. They discuss the kind of involvement that will be necessary if this play is to be a success, and each of them describes his particular schedule and responsibilities that will have effect on the rehearsal schedule. Then the rehearsal schedule is set, with the exact days and exact times of rehearsals through to the day of performance, which has also been approved by the cast. The schedule takes the major part of the time on that evening. Mr. Stanley explains that he had hoped to read through the play, but since there is not enough time he asks them to read through the play as many times as they can for the next rehearsal. (The rehearsals were scheduled generally on Monday, Wednesday, and Friday, with only a few variations from week to week and individual rehearsals with members of the cast).

Second Rehearsal—Wednesday, November 21:

Goals:　　　　　The first reading of the play for its story and its meaning.

Discussion of the play.

Minor changes of the cast.

Accomplished:　In the first reading there is no real concern with interpretation or characterization. After the reading there is an opportunity for questions from the actors and for the director's interpretation, plans for production, and especially for the director's suggestions for the most intelligent methods for the actors to work up their parts.

Third Rehearsal—Friday, November 23:

Goal:　　　　　To block Scene 1.

Accomplished: (Since the play is not divided into scenes as it is
written, the director divides the play into two
scenes for the purposes of blocking and rehearsing.) In blocking the movement of the actors on
stage it is necessary that they learn how to move
around in "the place" where the action takes place
and yet to be aware of the need for being seen
and heard by the audience. They should begin
to co-ordinate their bodily actions, their spoken
lines, and the ideas with which they are dealing.
When the blocking is completed for the first scene
it is set by immediately going through the scene
at least twice. The actors write down their movements in their scripts so that it will be easier to
remember them at the next rehearsal. At the end
of the first blocking rehearsal the actors are familiar with their movements onstage and with
the overall movement of the first scene.

Since the hall in which the play is to be performed is in constant use by various groups in the
church, it is necessary to rehearse elsewhere until
the last weeks of rehearsals. The director has
scheduled the use of another room and has marked
off a similar area which will give the same space
as the stage. This had to be worked out carefully with the church calendar in order to eliminate
any conflicts in the use of the hall.

SECOND WEEK
Fourth Rehearsal—Monday, November 26:
    Goal: To block Scene 2.
    Accomplished: Before this is done a brief run-through is made of
Scene 1 to be sure that the blocking is set, to al-
low for any changes the director wants to make,
and to get the actors working in the area in which
they will be blocking the second scene. The procedure for blocking Scene 2 is the same as that of
blocking Scene 1. The additional concern here is
that the climax and end of the play occur in this

scene. Therefore, the blocking is done with the end of the play in sight.

Fifth Rehearsal—Wednesday, November 28:

Goal: A complete run-through to set the blocking for the whole play; to get a feeling and understanding of the overall movement of the play.

Accomplished: The run-through reveals to the actors the unity of the play as a whole. This leads into the work on timing. (At this point all the rehearsals for the next two weeks are more or less the same kind of rehearsals, all of them working mainly on the timing—the co-ordination of speech and movement —working out all the many difficult spots in the play, attempting to make all of the action and direction work for the actors so that it becomes natural for them, discussing important words and ideas that must be communicated and how best to do this. During this time the lines and blocking are memorized. The director must insist on specific dates for this memorization.)

(It is during this time also that the director meets with the production people. The first meeting includes all the people involved. All of them must have a thorough understanding of the interpretation of the play and what is to be achieved in the completed production. Dates are assigned when the various production crews should have completed their work. The director tells when he wants them at rehearsals and warns them that the last week will be the one of major responsibility to the play. They must understand that the progress and ultimate success of the play now depends on their co-operation and their production of what is needed. Possibly the director has chosen an assistant director who will help him out in rehearsals and who will especially be responsible for production, checking with the production people, helping them do what they must, and being sure they meet their deadline. A devoted person as assistant director cannot only be an extremely important part of the entire production, but can also relieve the director of unnecessary responsibility so that his work with the actors can be more effective.)

THIRD WEEK

Seventh Rehearsal—Monday, December 3:

Goal: Scene 1 lines memorized.

Accomplished: The director insists that no scripts may be used and the actors are prompted as they miss lines. This scene is gone over several times. The director makes certain that there is no misunderstanding of lines. Any questions about meanings are discussed at this time.

FOURTH WEEK

Tenth Rehearsal—Monday, December 10:

Goal: Scene 2 lines memorized.

Accomplished: The same procedure as that used for Scene 1 is followed. (In the third and fourth weeks of rehearsals primary attention is given to the overall movement of the play: it should begin to run smoothly and should not drag; a certain pace should be felt and worked out until it becomes natural and dependable. Any elements necessary to co-ordinating the play, or bridging it, such as narration, music or other sounds, are introduced now and worked into the overall movement and mood of the play.)

During this next week, then, the demands of the play have doubled; therefore, the time spent on the show will necessarily double. Everyone should be well prepared for this period. The production people should be ready to go—now is the time to mount the show.

At the end of this week of rehearsals there is one week until the performance.

FIFTH WEEK

Thirteenth Rehearsal—Sunday, December 16:
    Goals: The set is up.
                     The cast rehearses on the complete set for the first time.
    Accomplished: Any changes in set, properties, et cetera are made.
                     The cast can feel what they will be working with.

Fourteenth Rehearsal—Monday, December 17:
    Goal: Technical work set.
    Accomplished: The lighting is tried out for the first time.
                     Technical rehearsals are always long and tedious and are more concerned with setting the technical aspects of the production than with the acting.

Fifteenth Rehearsal—Wednesday, December 19:
    Goals: Costumes.
                     Experimentation with the more complicated makeup requirements.
    Accomplished: The costumes are completed and fitted to the actors outside the regular rehearsal time, for the rehearsals must be devoted to putting the various elements to work, trying them out under lights, and letting the actors become familiar with their clothes. Doing as much of the experimentation as possible at this time will eliminate further stopping and interruption in other rehearsals that should be devoted to polishing the play.
                     The following rehearsal period is the most rigid and intensified period of work on the play.

Sixteenth Rehearsal—Thursday, December 20:
    Goal: Line rehearsal.
    Accomplished: The director is concerned with the actual text of the play—checking for correctness, emphasis on important factors in delivering lines, re-emphasis on the important places in the dialogue. He then lets the actors go early—they need the rest!

Seventeenth Rehearsal—Friday, December 21:
    Goal: Run-through with production details.

Accomplished: A complete, careful run-through with complete costumes and technical work is conducted. A few people are invited as a try-out audience. They comment on the production and the director takes advantage of any valuable suggestions. The visitors are dismissed and the cast goes back over the rough places that need work.

Eighteenth Rehearsal—Saturday, December 22:

Goal: Dress rehearsal.

Accomplished: The final, polished rehearsal is conducted as a preview for a few people invited just like the Friday audience. Preview audiences can be extremely valuable to amateur actors though they may become problems as far as the director is concerned. They do, however, make "opening nights" a less frightening experience, and they give the actors an idea of the audience response to expect from the play.

SIXTH WEEK

The Performance—Sunday, December 23:

Goal: Curtain at 8:00 on an artistic performance.

Accomplished: (The wise director calls his cast and his production people at just the right time before the performance. He must not insist that they come so early that they wear themselves out before the performance, yet they must have time enough to dress and be made up at a comfortable pace and not be rushed before the performance begins.)
                 Performance!

Chapter XII

THE PRODUCTION

A. Organizing for Production

THE ACTUAL BUSINESS OF CHOOSING AND PRODUCING A PLAY WILL REQUIRE organization similar to the following:

1. Director
2. Play-choosing committee
3. Casting committee
4. Technical director and production staff

A. Art director	E. Lighting crew
B. Building crew	F. Costume crew
C. Stage manager and stage crew	G. Makeup crew
D. Properties crew	

5. Business committee

A. Business manager	D. House
B. Ticket committee	E. Program
C. Publicity	

6. Prompter

1. Director. (See The Director and Directing, pp. 129-36.)

2. The play-choosing committee: The duties of the play-choosing committee have already been listed. (See Chapter IX.) The members of this committee should be reading plays constantly and should be storing away suggestions for other projects. They should be on the alert for names of plays that groups in other churches are producing. Church papers are an excellent source for this kind of information. The director always works closely with the play-choosing committee. His recommendation of plays should receive first attention, and he should be consulted before any plays are suggested to the group for production.

3. The casting committee (three persons and the director): The casting committee should act in an advisory capacity. Its first business is to see that on the date set for the tryout as many candidates as possible appear. Everyone with any ability should be urged to tryout. The committee can be of great help to the director in seeing that casting is done with all consideration and fairness. The director should have the final decision about any candidate. Because he is to direct, he must be able to work with the people in the cast. The committee should never try to dictate to the director or try to prejudice him. The group must always keep in mind that the production of the play in the best possible manner is the goal of the project. All effort should be bent toward that end.

Casting should not be considered final until after several rehearsals have been held. A person may read well in tryouts and yet have nothing to give in rehearsals. Several candidates may be chosen for the same part, and the best person selected early in the rehearsals. If the spirit of the group is right each person will find his place to work. In the co-operative venture of the church production of a play each job is of utmost importance.

4. The technical director and the production staff: This group turns the backstage wheels. The technical director is chosen by the production staff and the director. Next to the director the job of the technical director is most important. He is responsible to the director for all aspects of the technical production. The production staff (chairmen of the various crews) is responsible to the technical director for each member's particular part of the work. The technical director must be the integrator of the production. He follows the play script during rehearsals. Next to the director, he knows the play most thoroughly. Consequently, he is responsible for helping to make the director's promptbook—the complete record of the production showing all movement and stage business used, light plots, ground plots, costume and makeup charts. The stage manager is responsible to the technical director for the co-operation of the crews.

A. The art director may design both the set and the costumes, but usually two people are secured to design the sets and the costumes. When the set and costumes are not designed, he creates the ideas for whatever costumes and sets are used. If costumes are rented or borrowed he makes sure they are right. His job is to see that the scenery, properties, and costumes are in good taste and are historically authentic.

B. The building crew is responsible to the technical director and the art director for the building of the scenery. When no scenery is to be built, the duty of the crew is to furnish the screens, drapes, and set pieces that may be used. For church productions this committee needs to be ingenious. Many times the facilities for producing a play do not allow scenery to be constructed. Often the play will not permit movable scenery. In these cases the committee will devise ways and means of representing the scene and of changing it. Excellent books on production are available for learning ways of constructing scenery. Persons mechanically inclined or those adept in the use of tools should be members of this committee.

C. The stage manager and stage crew are responsible for placing the set and for changing the scenery. The stage manager is responsible to the director for getting the stage ready for all action. He picks and directs a stage crew, whose business it is to follow his direction in changing the setting. He must be a good manager and must be systematic in his work. The smoothness of a production will depend upon him. He should have a floor plan for each scene and should organize his stage crew so that scenery can be changed in the quickest possible time.

D. The properties crew should get a list of all the properties from the director. Properties are all the movable things used in a production other than scenery. These are both set pieces and hand properties. The list should show when the props are needed. The committee should assemble the props early and should have them available for the cast as soon as possible. Any prop that has to be "worked" should be tried out in the rehearsals to see that it is in good working order. The chairman of the committee should be artistically inclined.

E. The lighting crew is extremely important in the whole setup. If at all possible, someone trained in lighting should be secured as chairman of this crew. Certainly care should be taken to see that no unauthorized person touches the lights. The physical dangers are at once apparent, and fire may result from ignorant meddling.

F. The costume crew may be large or small depending on the number and period of the costumes. A good chairman can often borrow costumes. If he has artistic ability he can make them cheaply.

The costumes should be ready sufficiently early so that the actors can become thoroughly familiar with them and can feel at home in them. There should be few last-minute changes and remodeling.

G. The makeup crew must be organized so that at the last minute it functions smoothly and speedily. Before the dress rehearsal the committee should make whatever experiments are necessary. During the dress rehearsal the committee should sit in the audience and note any changes that need to be made under lighting. Religious drama often requires difficult makeup, and the committee should start work and experimentation very early in the rehearsal period. Several good books on makeup are available.

5. The business committee (the business manager and his assistants): The business management of a play is obviously important. Here is an opportunity for those who may not be artistically inclined but whose talents and interests lie in the field of business.

An estimate of the costs should be made and a budget drawn up. The director's fee, the royalty, the printing, the production costs, and the house expenses must be included in the estimate. A reserve fund should always be kept for emergencies such as loss and breakage. Every person spending money should get a receipt for what he spends. This should be kept with his statement to be turned in to the business manager when the production is over. The business manager should submit a complete and final report of all money taken in and expended. All bills, including royalty, should be paid promptly.

A. The business manager must be the head of a three-ring circus —tickets, publicity, and house. He must be a person with clever ideas, yet he must always be practical in his dealing with the rest of the organization. If tickets are to be sold he should map out a campaign for publicity and ticket-selling. He must also work with the entire stage staff in keeping down the costs of production.

B. The ticket committee has entire responsibility for the sale of tickets. Never make the ticket sale a nuisance in the church. It is an important part of the process of play production and should be kept on a dignified plane.

C. Publicity: A good publicity chairman and committee are invaluable assets to a performance. Publicity in a church should be an educational process. The committee should know the play thoroughly, should attend some rehearsals, and should understand enough about the play in its period to be intelligent about it. Their effort should be to make people want to come because attendance will be worthwhile. The facts about the play, the plot, comedy, characters, will make good sales talk. Interesting news about the director, actors, and stage crews will also make good material. Bulletins, posters, letters, newspapers, and talks should all be used. A short, colorful scene may be presented before organizations to show something of the play's charm and value. The publicity people should be alive to every opportunity to give news of the play. Experience in news writing can be gained in this way. To secure newspaper publicity feed the paper a series of articles giving different aspects of the production. Give a general idea of the play first. Then follow with an article about the cast, the director, the artists, and the stage crew emphasizing all the types of persons taking part. Names make news. Keep some new ones for each article. Keep the play before the people and make them conscious of it at all times.

D. House: The house committee takes care of everything in the auditorium on the night of the performance except the sale of tickets, which is in the hands of the ticket committee or business manager. Ushers may make the whole performance seem better to the audience. Neat, alert young people should usher. The house manager should also see that the auditorium is properly ventilated.

E. Program: If a printed program is to be used be sure that someone is appointed to supervise the printing. Every name should be spelled correctly and each person serving in any capacity should be listed. Each person's contribution is important, and everyone should be given credit. Drama in the church should not feature actors above the others in the co-operative venture. Use the largest type for the name of the play. Never feature a player. Give the director credit on a separate line. Be careful not to make advertisements in a program a community nuisance. In most communities this should not be undertaken at all. Allow a small amount in the budget for the programs and make them as attractive as possible.

6. The prompter is to note the action as it is mapped out. He should write it down in the promptbook so that the action will be recorded

in case an actor forgets, another actor is substituted, or a dispute concerning action arises. The prompter should give undivided attention to this book. This is an important job; consequently a very intelligent person is required. The prompter must be present at all rehearsals. He should also note pauses in the dialogue and be careful not to prompt unless the actor has really forgotten his lines. His promptbook becomes a valuable part of the drama library when the play has been produced.

In drama in the church curtain calls should not be customary, and under no circumstances should gifts to the cast or the director be passed over the footlights or be made obvious backstage.

After the play has been produced, the stage cleared, the properties returned, the scenery and costumes stored away, and the whole house set in order, the director and his organization will want to check up on the results. In a church performance there is little chance for professional criticism, but every church organization should plan for an accounting. Just as a complete financial statement is necessary, so it is also desirable to look at the net results after a performance. This may be done in several ways.

A few competent persons should be asked to give a criticism of the production. The director and cast, as well as the producing group, should be told that this is to be done for the benefit of future productions and for the education of the persons taking part. If the persons selected do not want to appear to give their criticisms they should be asked to write them.

A meeting should be called within a week after the final performance. The president of the group, or some other official of the church, should state the purpose of the meeting. Then the cast, the crew, and the director, together with members from the audience, should be asked to state their criticisms as honestly and as frankly as possible. If this is done in the right spirit it will be a thoroughly educational process. The criticism of those invited or of anyone interested should then be given. These should be carefully discussed and digested. Suggestions as to what was wrong and what can be done to better the next production should be considered with great care.

The whole process of producing a play in the church should be an experience of religious proportions. As a co-operative experience it gives to the participants the opportunity of learning to work with a group, of being able to take directions, of being creative both artistically and mechanically, of playing together, and finally of learning to take criticism to improve one's self. It should be a genuinely educational process fraught with happy experiences and worthwhile results. Until it reaches this standard, drama in the church is not achieving its real ends nor is it being the activity that it rightly deserves to be.

B. Scenery

The art of scenic production has never been more advanced than at the present time. It is the work of specialized artists as well as famous painters such as Pablo Picasso and Salvador Dali. The scenic designer makes visible what the dramatist has in mind for the setting of the play. In this process of visualization he is joined by the director of the play who sees the action within the limits of the stage or playing space. The scene designer, therefore, is limited by the original idea of the playwright and the need for movement in the direction of the play.

In the older concept of scenery the stage was dressed to represent the scene by scene painting. A backdrop was painted to represent the perspective of a forest or a hall while the flats in the wings were painted to give a continuing sense of the place, allowing for the acting area with its need for such stationary props to fulfill the actualization of what came to be known as the set. In recent years the scene designer working with the light designer has inherited a much more different role. Robert Edmond Jones calls scenery the "environment" factor.

Modern conceptions of scene design date from the work of Gordon Craig, who in the first quarter of this century maintained that scenery should be the visual expression of the dynamic spirit of a play.[1] The other great pioneer of stage space design was Adolphe Appia, who, along with Craig, cleared the stage for vistas, for light, and for action that was free and flowing, adding to the vitality of the action. The contemporary artists in scene design have followed these lines, freeing the stage to present best the action of the play as it is visualized by the director. The concept of scenery as establishing *visual environment* dates from Appia and Craig and it has been agreed to by most scene designers. The idea of environment proposes the placing of a scene and the imaginative suggestion of the place without actually imitating it. In this use of scenery, the spectator is made to feel the place without actually having it shown.

Another contribution that scenery can make to the action of a play is the presentation of the idea without the forms so that a style is achieved. Some character or style of the play is given visual representation in the scenery. Scenery of this stylized nature was used in both Eugene O'Neill's *The Hairy Ape* and *The Emperor Jones*.

Contemporary artists are also freeing the stage of representational scenery so that the playing space is indicated by set pieces or architectural forms such as walls, platforms, and steps. In such space-staging the actor is released to use the freedom in space, but he is called upon to make his action much more telling because he is without the benefit of pieces that might define for him the environmental assets of realistic scenery. He may have little to lean on, nothing to support his words, and he will need to control his body since its movements are much more obvious when they are "in the open."

In the Greek and Elizabethan theater there was little or no scene building. The actors played against a background which probably was the same from scene to scene. This type of setting has again become popular in the contemporary use of outdoor and arena stages. Many schools present plays on a stage that is defined by a cyclorama or curtains against which scenes are played. This "accepted environment" is used for many plays of different types.

What is important to remember is that the scene designer is faced with the limitations of the size of the playing area, that he must suggest by his scenery the place and the mood of the play, as well as its time and its opportunity to allow the actor to create the scene that is called for in the script of the play.

Informal staging, used now in theater-in-the-round, is not informal. It may be more flexible staging because it is viewed from many angles. It is often more difficult than ordinary picture-frame staging since it must allow movement in a variety of directions and allow actors to face the audience which is often on all sides of the playing space. Picture-frame staging does not expose a room by taking off the fourth wall, as is so often suggested. Even picture-frame staging is theatrical in that it exposes a room to the best advantage to an audience looking at one side of it. Even David Belasco could not make an audience believe that one side of a room had been removed. The room had been arranged by the scene designer to allow actors within it and to show this action to the audience.

In arena staging or theater-in-the-round walls disappear and scenery as such is scarcely ever used. This type of setting uses stationary and movable props and depends on lighting for the definition of the playing space. It can be used to great advantage in parish halls and in rooms where a stage is not possible.

Screens, in two-or-three-joint sections, are useful for chancel drama. They can be moved easily, set at a variety of angles, and arranged in interesting designs. They can be made of profile or fiberboard. They should be painted some neutral color, perhaps the walnut finish of the chancel furniture or a shade of gray or tan. They are often used for the mounting of pictures or hangings. Their size should be determined by the size of the playing areas and the auditorium. Screens must be sufficiently wide to stand firmly when jointed with another section and should be sufficiently heavy not to be in danger of upsetting should they be hit by an actor. They should be thick enough to prevent light from behind seeping through. Because of their extreme flexibility screens are very useful for church drama.

All scenery and properties used in space-staging should be so planned that they can be placed before the service begins. There should be as little shifting of screens or set pieces during the performance as possible.

It is important that a satisfactory place be designated for the storing of all equipment. This storage room or closet should be kept orderly. Crews should be trained to return each piece of equipment to its proper place. A good director will help his crews to feel pride in the systematic way in which all scenery, properties, costumes, and lights are cared for.

C. Properties

Properties are those parts of equipment which are used by actors and which decorate or complete the setting. The business of the property chairman and his crew is to gather props and see that they are in the hands of the actors at the proper times. If a play has a large number of properties and a large cast, the surest way of supplying an actor with his hand props is to assign a crew member to be individually responsible for one or more members of the cast. After the performance the property crew should see that all borrowed items are returned. Those properties bought or owned by the group must be listed and stored for possible future use.

Properties should not be merely gathered at the time of a play; they should be obtained whenever they are available. In the spring and in the fall it is a good idea to put a notice in the church bulletin saying the property and costume committees would welcome all donations of hats, canes, furniture, clothing, and white elephants. Auction sales, salvage stores, old trunks, and attics are all good sources of properties. Collecting and care of properties can become an interesting and worthwhile facet of dramatic productions in the church.

D. Costumes

Milton Smith calls costumes "scenery worn by actors," and certainly many of the principles determining the use of scenery in chancel drama are applicable to the use of costumes. In chancel drama costumes should be as simple as possible providing they portray the character.

Difficult costumes should be worn by actors in rehearsal as early as possible. Many times biblical plays are ruined by actors who are embarrassed and self-conscious about their costumes. The clothing must seem as natural for them to wear as their lines in character are to speak.

In biblical plays a great deal of attention must be given to costumes. Costumes should be authentic; however, authenticity should not be carried to an absurd extreme. Dress that causes a congregation to laugh thwarts the purpose of religious drama to give greater understanding and appreciation for nations and peoples.

The church groups will want and need a costume wardrobe. As in the case of properties the alert group will collect costumes from the church members, the community, and rummage sales.

E. Makeup

In chancel drama a minimum of makeup should be used. Makeup is used to accentuate the features so that from a distance they will appear natural. When makeup is overdone it detracts from rather than makes for naturalness. The intensity of the lighting, the distance of the actors from the audience, and the difference in the facial characteristics of the actor from those of the person he is portraying will determine the amount and accentuation of makeup. Superficial manuals on play production are not the source of satisfactory guidance in the art of makeup. Some of the capable practitioners of this art have thorough books on the subject. With the aid of these books the amateur may learn a great deal about the techniques of makeup. Beards, wigs, and graying of hair are all dangerous in unskilled hands. Bad jobs will call attention to themselves and will spoil the effectiveness of the drama. Rather than risk an incompetent makeup job, a group should work without makeup. For difficult makeups there should be much experimentation. Actors using wigs and beards should wear them in as many rehearsals as possible. The director will need to watch carefully to see that actors do not appear in performance with their own jewelry or makeup. For example, a director must see that a prophet of the Old Testament does not wear a wrist watch and that Mary the Mother of Jesus does not have lacquered fingernails.

F. Lighting

The lighting of a play is perhaps more difficult than any other phase of its production, and it determines the effectiveness of the presentation perhaps more than any other aspect. Under proper illumination cheap material in costumes may look rich. Lighting, enabling one to see facial expressions, makes the difference between interest and dullness. The correct use of lighting can make for power in any performance. It is not a dress rehearsal consideration. The lighting facilities of an auditorium will figure in choosing, directing and acting the play.

Effective and safe lighting demands the services of an electrician who knows stage-lighting and the lighting needs of the particular play. A lighting designer must have experience enough to know what can and cannot be done in stage-lighting in order to achieve desired effects. He must know the mood, purpose, and quality of the play. He must have attended enough rehearsals so that he knows the location and size of playing areas and the exits and entrances. He must study the ground plan of the playing area. It is conceivable that a group might have one person who fulfills these three needs, but usually it takes more skills than one person possesses.

Those in charge of lighting should insist upon having the auditorium for technical rehearsals. They must test their lighting from various parts of the auditorium and be sure that the light is not so harsh or so weak that the audience will have to strain to see.

The purpose of lighting is to make the play visible. The person untrained in lighting often makes the play almost invisible. Care should be taken that, while a mood is maintained through the lighting, the actors remain easily visible. Lighting also serves to establish the time and locale and to intensify and objectify the mood of the scene. For example, an abundance of straw-colored, surprise-pink, and steel-blue light will tell an audience that it is daytime—and the more straw color in the light, the more cheer in the mood. Other colors of light, of course, convey other times of day and other moods.

In space-staging lighting serves as a curtain. It also focuses the audience's attention, guides their eyes, and affects their feelings.

Specific illumination is desirable for drama in the chancel. For this type of illumination the lighting instrument is so constructed that it controls the shape and size of the pool of light which it casts. The spotlight, which gives specific illumination, is the most useful piece of lighting equipment for the church. Lighting equipment is expensive; nevertheless, because good lighting can make poor costuming and scenery effective, and poor lighting can destroy the effectiveness of good costuming and scenery, it should be the primary production consideration. Professional-theater lighting equipment is most desirable. It is far better to have one safe, efficient, and dependable piece of equipment than a whole collection of shoddy, inefficient, carelessly constructed equipment. The technical director should get catalogues from dependable manufacturers of theatrical lighting equipment.

Groups should add to their lighting equipment. A goal might be to add a spotlight with each new play or one every six months. It is far wiser to spend money for a good piece of lighting equipment than for elaborate costumes or sets which may be used only a few times.

Above all, lighting equipment for the church should be flexible. A lighting instrument which may be used in only one way and for one purpose is a loss. For example, it would be foolish to buy floodlights, border lights, and footlights. By removing the lens of a spotlight, we have a floodlight. By using a battery of spots, we have borders or foots. In addition to being flexible, equipment should be light in weight, durable, and should give as much light as possible for its size and wattage. In time, good cables should be bought to replace the traditional extension cord. Colored gelatines should be bought in quantities rather than just enough for each play. Stands, clamps, and any special rigging needed to solve the lighting problems of a particular auditorium should be secured. Extra fuses should be on hand at all times.

Quantity and quality of lighting instruments are not the sole solution to the difficult task of lighting chancel drama. The architecture of most churches makes the placement of lighting equipment a real problem. Only through the ingenuity of the light crew working in their own auditorium can the final solution be found. The following suggestions, however, may be helpful to a few groups. Crosslighting, originating from the sides and converging at the playing area, is more desirable than frontlighting. It may be that in some churches both cross- and frontlighting will be desirable and possible.

If a church has a balcony which follows around the side walls of the auditorium, lighting is comparatively simple. Powerful spots may be used opposite each other at the front of the church; their beams may meet and pass through each other when they reach the playing areas. If a church has a balcony only across the rear of the auditorium, spots at both sides or a single powerful spot, centrally placed, may serve the purpose. If a church has no balcony and if there are no pillars or ceilings from which spots may be rigged, light instruments may be clamped to stands and placed behind screens at each side of the playing area. If the playing area is sufficiently elevated, spots may be placed between the chancel rail and the first row of pews; or in some instances spots may be used on standards placed in the front pews. Masking of all visible instruments must be effective! Lighting from the sides or rear of a balcony or from the front of the auditorium will throw shadows upon the wall back of the playing area. Unless a shadow is used purposefully and dramatically, it must be eliminated. Otherwise, the flitting, grotesque shadows of actors will destroy all possibility of concentration upon the play. One way of solving this problem is to throw light upon the back wall. Spots with lenses removed or bucket lights can be used for this purpose. If the play is such that some kind of hanging is desired on the back wall, it will serve to absorb the shadows.

Because outlets may be great distances from the instruments, many cords and cables will be needed; where they cross entrances and exits they should be tacked down and covered with carpet.

It can be seen that the lighting of drama must be planned and experimented with long before the presentation. Nothing should be left to chance. If it is impossible for the person who operates the switchboard to see the actors or hear the cues, he must be given much practice in taking the cues from someone else. Even though the operator has had thorough rehearsal, the tenseness of the performance may cause him to forget. Cue sheets should be made for lights. Diagrams and charts should be worked out to show which instruments control which playing areas. The connections and switches controlling all instruments should be as simple as possible. It is highly desirable to have all instruments as well as auditorium lights controlled from one place. In some instances the building of a portable switchboard may be necessary. Circuits should be so set up that the throwing of one or perhaps two switches will make all the light changes necessary for one change of scene. Care given to the lining up of circuits makes for smoothness and infallibility of lighting. During dress rehearsals when lighting is used the light chairman should sit in the auditorium to check the lighting. There will be times when, due to lack of equipment or the angles or distances from which instruments are rigged, acting areas may have to be shifted in order to keep all actors in the light pool or to have sufficient light on their faces. The light chairman should also be alert to check upon the actor who has not developed a sense of the importance of staying within the lighted areas.

Lighting like scenery is right in proportion to its subtle intensification, its unobtrusiveness, and its lack of theatrical effects. Lighting should be an integral part of the whole composition of the chancel drama. Attention should be given to getting the feel for the right lighting changes between the end of a play and the time for the audience to leave. It may be that the same lighting is used after the drama which was used before the play began. Then after a few moments the coming on of a few wall lights and lights in the vestibule will indicate to the audience that they may leave when they wish.

At times it may seem as if there is little to show for the infinite patience, the perseverance, the hours of labor, put into the technical aspects of dramatic production in the chancel. To many people there is little to show for all the hours involved. Yet because the work is concentrated in building moods and feelings, production for chancel drama can be satisfying and rewarding.

Notes

[1] Craig's main contribution is recorded in his book On the Art of the Theatre (New York: Dodd, Mead & Company, 1925).

GENERAL BOOKS ON THEATER AND DRAMA ON WHAT IS HAPPENING IN PRESENT-DAY DRAMA AND THEATER

This bibliography represents the thinking of writers who are evaluating the current state of the theater and the changing techniques of authors. Paperbacks are suggested when available.

Abel, Lionel. *Metatheatre*. New York: Hill & Wang, 1963. A statement of a new form of drama replacing the so-called problem play.

Armstrong, William, ed., *Experimental Drama*. Chester Springs, Pa.: Dufour Editions, 1963. A stimulating source book.

Artaud, Antonin. *The Theatre and Its Double*. New York: Grove Press, Evergreen Book (E-127), 1958. Theatre and Culture, Balinese and Oriental Theatre; The Theatre of Cruelty (1st Manifesto); The Theatre of Cruelty (2nd Manifesto); In Memoriam: Antonin Artaud by Maurice Saillet.

Baxter, Kay M. *Contemporary Theatre and the Christian Faith*. New York and Nashville: Abingdon Press, 1967. Plays by Beckett, Graham Greene, Anouilh, Camus, Whiting, Miller, Williams, Osborne, Fry, Henri Bernanos analyzed in the light of theater criticism and religious understanding.

Bentley, Eric. *Theatre of Commitment*. New York: Atheneum, 1967. An excellent summation of the contemporary theater.

Brecht, Bertolt. *Brecht on Theatre*. Edited by J. Willett. New York: Hill & Wang (D42), 1964. The major critical writings on theater and aesthetics showing Brecht's ideas as they developed.

Brustein, Robert. *The Theatre of Revolt*. Boston: Little, Brown, 1964. A paperback. Studies of eight playwrights in rebellion and their influence on contemporary theater.

Cohn, Ruby, ed. *Casebook on Waiting for Godot*. New York: Grove Press, Evergreen Book (E-441), 1967. A paperback. The impact of Beckett's modern classic: reviews, reflections, and interpretations.

Cole, Toby. *Playwrights on Playwrighting*. New York: Hill & Wang, 1960. A paperback.

Cole, Toby and Chinoy, Krich, Helen, eds. *Actors on Acting*. New York: Crown, 1949. *Directors on Directing*. Indianapolis: Bobbs-Merrill, 1963. A paperback.

Corrigan, Robert W., and Rosenberg, J. L. *Context and Craft of Drama*. Chicago: Chandler, Science Research Associates, 1964. A paperback. Critical essays on the nature of drama and theater.

Driver, Tom F. *Romantic Quest and Modern Query*. New York: Delacorte Press, 1970. A history of the modern theater.

Ellison, Jerome. *God on Broadway*. Richmond, Va.: John Knox, 1971. A paperback. An analysis of the God theme in plays such as *The Great God Brown, Tiny Alice, Fiddler on the Roof, Hair*.

Esslin, Martin. *The Theatre of the Absurd*. Garden City, N.Y.: Doubleday,

Anchor (A279), n.d. The best summary of the absurd plays. Excellent and clarifying commentary.

Gheon, Henri. *Art of the Theatre.* New York: Hill & Wang Drama Books (D26), 1961. Ideas of the man who has written the best religious plays with a sense of humor.

Gottfried, Martin. *A Theatre Divided: The Postwar American Stage.* Boston: Little, Brown, 1967. Right wing (commercial) and left wing theater. Opinionated but intelligent comments on the stage and its future—arguing that both wings are needed in the theater of the future.

Grossvogel, David. *Blasphemers: The Theatre of Brecht, Ionesco, Beckett, Genet.* Ithaca, N.Y.: Cornell University Press, 1965. A paperback. A reasoned discussion of the dramatists and their works.

Johnson, Albert. *Directing Methods.* South Brunswick, N.J.: A. S. Barnes, 1970. The personal directing methods of an experienced director.

Johnson, Albert and Johnson, Bertha. *Drama for Junior High.* South Brunswick and New York: A. S. Barnes, 1971. A rare book in that it is the only one published especially for junior high.

Jones, Robert Edmond. *The Dramatic Imagination: Reflections and Speculations on the Art of the Theatre.* 5th printing. New York: Theatre Arts Books, 1941. "Keep in your souls some images of magnificence."

Kershaw, John. *The Present Stage: New Directions in the Theatre Today.* London: Collins Fontana Books (1417), 1966. Based on ABC Television Series. Osborn, Wesker, Frisch, Pinter, Ionesco, Beckett. Excellent analysis of one representative play by each author.

Kirby, Michael, ed. *Happenings: An Illustrated Anthology.* New York: E. P. Dutton, 1966. Scripts and productions by Jim Dine, Red Grooms, Allan Kaprow, Claes Oldenburg, Robert Whitman. Illuminating introduction and notes on productions.

Kline, Peter. *The Theatre Student: Playwriting.* New York: John Rosen, 1970. For the beginning student. The shaping of plot and dialogue.

Mander, John. *The Writer and Commitment.* Chester Springs, Pa.: Dufour Editions, 1961. A provocative statement on a subject that has immediate importance.

Rowe, Kenneth Thorpe. *A Theatre in Your Head.* New York: Funk & Wagnalls, 1960. The reading of plays; visualization, experiencing, understanding, and evaluating the play.

Schechner, Richard. *Public Domain: Essays on the Theatre.* New York: Avon Discus, 1970. Of interest to all who wonder what is happening to the theater.

Shank, Theodore J., ed. *A Digest of 500 Plays.* New York: The Crowell-Collier Press, 1963. Plot outlines and production notes.

Siks, Geraldine. *Creative Dramatics.* New York: Harper, 1958. The theories of the leading practicing authority.

Siks, Geraldine, and Dunnington, H. B., eds. *Children's Theatre and Creative Dramatics.* Seattle, Washington: University of Washington, 1961. A restatement with valuable discussion of the children's theater.

Spolin, Viola. *Improvisation for the Theatre.* Evanston, Ill.: Northwestern University Press, 1963. One of the best books available to directors of drama in the local church.

Steiner, George. *The Death of Tragedy.* New York: Hill & Wang Drama Books

(YD35), 1961. A paperback. Suggests that tragedy as a vision of man is outdated. Studies the efforts of serious dramatists to treat the newer subjects.

Styan, J. L. *The Dramatic Experience: A Guide to the Reading of Plays.* New York: Cambridge University Press, 1965. Suggests what the dramatic experience is, how it differs from the novel or poem, what dramatic effects are, and how they are created. Historical development. Charming illustrations by David Gentleman.

Taylor, James R. *Anger and After.* Baltimore: Penguin, Pelican (A641), 1964. A paperback. Treatment of British dramatists who emerged in the fifties.

Taylor, John Russell. *Rise and Fall of the Well-made Play.* New York: Hill & Wang, 1967. A book on the transition of technique in drama.

Ward, Winifred. *Playmaking with Children.* 2d ed. New York: Appleton-Century, Crofts, 1957. The original and definitive book on the subject.

Ward, Winifred. *Theatre for Children.* Rev. ed. Anchorage, Ky.: Children's Theatre Press, 1958. Out of the experience of the founder of the Evanston Children's Theatre.

Wellwarth, George. *The Theatre of Protest and Paradox.* New York: New York University, n.d. The avant-garde in French, German, British, and United States drama.

Recordings on the Theater

Album of Stars, as presented by the American National Theatre and Academy. Decca (DL9002,9009). Great moments from great plays as interpreted by a score of distinguished actors.

Directing a Play, by Tyrone Guthrie. Folkways (FL 9840). A lecture on the director and the script, the production, and the staging.

Towards a New Theatre, by Robert Edmond Jones. Vocarium (VD 1000) 2 records. Lecture by an outstanding theatre artist.

Arthur Miller speaking on and reading from *The Crucible* and *Death of a Salesman.* Spoken Arts (704). A distinguished playwright interprets his work.

Sean O'Casey reading from his works. Caedmon (TC 1012). Selections from *Juno and the Paycock, Inishfallen, Fare Thee Well*, and *Pictures in the Hallway.*

Talking About Theatre. London (5717). Taped interviews by outstanding figures in British theatre: Noel Coward, Albert Finney, Peter Hall, Sean Kenny, Siobhan McKenna, Harold Pinter, Sybil Thorndike, Kenneth Tynan, and Peter Ustinov.

John Van Druten. Westminister (718). The playwright speaking on and reading from *The Art of Playwriting, The Voice of the Turtle, The Druid Circle, I Am a Camera*, and *I've Got Sixpence.*

Tennessee Williams reading from his works. Caedmon (TC 1005). A selection from the writings of the distinguished playwright.

Dear Audience, by Blanche Yurka. Folkways (FL 9841 and 9842). A guide to the enjoyment of theater with scenes from great plays presented. Commentary by Blanche Yurka.